Dedication

To my father, whose example taught me the fun of business, to my mother, who expertly kept the supporting order, and to Ed, who taught entrepreneuring like it is.

Acknowledgements

Many thanks to Catherine Hess for being the magnet who brought this book out of me by her willingness to be my student. Thanks to Duane Schau for showing me that a sensitive, people-oriented, intuitive man can make it as a computer consultant in a large institution. Thanks to Kent MacPherson for having the skill to make his business a huge success and being the first man I have met who knew when to stop expanding. And enormous thanks to Dwight Sands for his patience and willingness to be my teacher as I learn how to communicate with the computer.

Disclaimer

This book is designed as a basic map for bringing ideas into material reality. It is based upon the opinion and experience of the author. Neither the publisher nor the author are engaged in the business of providing legal or accounting services. If legal or other specific expert assistance is required, please seek out a competent professional.

Contents

List of Charts

Introduction

"How might I bring about a simple, harmonious daily life of integrity, joy, deep loving experience, and a reasonable security on the material plane in the present day society without hurting Mother Earth or denying my personal values and creativity?" This was the question I carefully framed and asked myself again and again until I discovered the answer. I believe you are asking this question too.

After years of observing talented and caring people's lives being wasted in mediocre jobs which devour their time and energy and dull their creativity for a meager wage, I decided to attempt to catalog the path of building a business which encourages the expression of the true you.

Because of the tremendous positive response I received from the publication of the **Medicine Woman Inner Guidebook** and the **Medicine Woman Tarot,** I know many women and men are crying for a vision of a way to create the sane world we all desire. People want the nitty-gritty of how to go about making the changes they see are needed while still providing for their families and meeting their obligations. Yet many intuitive and creative people will not be reached by the average business how-to book.

It is time to tap these talents. This book is for the creatively endowed and the financially below average. It attempts to clear the path for action on your positive ideas.

Ancient systems of harmony underlie the sound business advice offered in this workbook. By following the steps herein, you can immediately begin to activate your special talents and move toward financial reward while keeping in tune with the spirit of life.

This book is for you, the intuitive, loving individual who may have trouble coming to terms with money. It is for the kindhearted, the visionary, the innocent of worldly ways, and the idealist. It is meant to say "you can" and to show you exactly how. It is not meant to gloss over real work and complex problems. It is not a positive thinking manual. Yet it is designed to make business an affirming and fun experience even while you carry out the most commonplace tasks.

I hope you enjoy it. The 22 Accomplishments correlate with a timeless system of attunement to the seasons and cycles of life, the tarot. This system has worked for me, connecting the spiritual and material worlds and helping me to see the natural progression of challenges and successes which are nature's way. My income has doubled each year for the last four years and my life is rich with Spirit. For these blessings, I am truly thankful. May your life be enhanced by this path.

Meeting the Boss

Look in the mirror. This is who you are going to be working for from now on. Whether you are self-employed, employed by someone else, or trying to decide which way to go, if you can treat the situation as if you are in charge of your life, soon you will be.

Business is a part of the path of balance. It is the art of fair exchange. Anyone striving to bring good medicine to the world of today must acknowledge the need to return to a state of living in balance. In native traditions, the path of balance is depicted symbolically by the Medicine Wheel, a circle divided into four quadrants, one for each direction: north, east, south, and west. Each direction brings forth a teaching about life.

The North tells how to relate to material things, objects made of earth substances like metal, wood, and all that comes from the body of the planet. The earth is recognized as a living being in this system. To remind us of this, I shall speak of her with a capital "E." Earth is matter, Earth is mother of all material things. Thus material reality, even money, must be respected as a part of her being.

The East tells how to use creative energy and inspiration. Being the direction of the dawn, East awakens us and revitalizes our desire to bring forth something new, something better. East on the Medicine Wheel relates to the season of spring, the time of planting seeds for future harvest. As we observe nature in her seasonal cycle around the wheel, we can see that in harmony with her, we, too, often feel a surge of excitement for beginning something every spring. East encourages us through the dawn of each day and the spring of each year to create.

> *I am assuming you would love to live a balanced life, one in which there is plenty of time to observe the seasons, to take in the sunset, to take a walk at midday just to feel the sun, to sleep in peace.*

The South comes along, bringing summer, and lets us know that we must focus that creative energy. Give it a direction. Move it through obstacles. The teaching of the South is, "Take charge." It takes the power of your personal will to get any idea off the ground, no matter how divinely inspired or wildly exciting. You must weed the garden, physically, mentally, emotionally. Leave only what you are trying to grow.

The West reminds us to then relax, take a look back. Enjoy the changes that inevitably occur. Everything begins, grows, flourishes for awhile, dies to that which comes next. Fall is the season of changing colors, falling leaves, nature letting go, just as you must let go. To live and work in balance, each day and each time of year as you are reminded by nature surrounding you, you must act in harmony with her. Take time to look over your accomplishments, give thanks for your resources and opportunities, and offer what you have done with them to a Greater Presence than yourself.

I am assuming you would love to live a balanced life, one in which there is plenty of time to observe the seasons, to take in the sunset, to take a walk at midday just to feel the sun, to sleep in peace. I also assume that you have responsibilities in the material world and would like to earn your living in a way that utilizes your talents, takes advantage of your creative ideas, and moves you toward your own goals. The Medicine Wheel teachings can help you do just that.

In this book, the teachings of the Medicine Wheel are divided into twenty-two lessons. They begin with "Planting the Seed" and take you all the way to "Dancing On Top of the World." I have personally doubled my income each year for the past four years using this system. And money was not my only goal. My goals were in accord with the Medicine Wheel, the seasons of life: to respect the Mother and her bountiful gifts, to allow my full creative expression, to stick to my chosen direction, and to make time to enjoy my life.

The system works. Now, let's get on with showing you how to use it to achieve the life you want through the work which pleases you.

Call Yourself A Shaman

Traditionally, a shaman enters the spiritual world and brings back power to the people. This is often a healing power. Today, our world is sick, parts of it are engulfed in poison, other parts are cancerously overgrown. It does not matter how you define the illness nor how much you believe in the patient's chances of recovery. You must do what you can. You want to do what you can.

Until now, you may not have realized that you had any power with which to heal. Perhaps you have never defined yourself as a medicine person of any kind. There was no need to. But now, as if you landed on an island and discovered the inhabitants were calling for help with no doctor at hand, you find you may be the only help available. In spite of your lack of specific medical training, you reach inside yourself to call upon all of your life experience, innate creativity, and sheer strength of will to do the very best you can. You are surprised with the results.

In your compassion and desire to achieve a beneficial result, a spiritual energy is called forth. You and this spirit cooperate fully. It uses every bit of your talent to bring about good. Whether you have realized it or not, this is the situation you are in right now.

The Earth needs your help. All of those who "should" be fixing her may be doing all they can, but it has not yet turned the situation around. The children of the future are holding out their hands, looking up at you with pleading eyes. "Please?" And in spite of your doubts about your abilities to pull it off, you say, "I will do my best."

> *No traditional shaman was ever separate from the daily trials and tribulations of her or his people. You are not separate from those of your world.*

This is how you must look at your job. The job we are going to create together for you as you read and do the exercises in this book. You will have to do a little magic. Call upon a spiritual power. Call it what you will. Begin by calling yourself a shaman. You need not define yourself to anyone else this way, but just allow yourself to imagine that maybe you do have a little access to powers you did not know were within or at your command.

On the other hand, this is not a magic book. It is not a "positive thinking" treatise. You cannot "have it all." I hope you do not want it all. I am trusting that you want a little more "reality" and practicality to combine with your hope for the future. No traditional shaman was ever separate from the daily trials and tribulations of her or his people. You are not separate from those of your world.

If you have thought of money and power as negative in themselves, the cause of social ills, you might benefit from a more positive attitude. Greed is the more accurate evil. Greed is taking without giving back.

In a word, imbalance. Greed does not necessarily have anything to do with how much you have but how little you give in return for it. Profit differs from greed in that it is simply a descriptive financial term for having enough money to continue putting forth your efforts. To continue giving back.

A shaman and a business person must both use power. To be a good shaman or business person you must recognize the form of the powers that be. Right now, that form is money. Money is the symbol for the powers that be, that is, the recognized and socially accepted symbol for status, success, intelligence, savvy, talent, charisma, knowledge, beauty, and luck.

You may have a different set of values. But the world still affects you because you are within it. You are surrounded by it. Your task, therefore, is not to try to escape (even if you could), but to gather the tools of "the enemy" and turn them to your/everyone's advantage. The swords into plowshares approach. Money as good medicine. The enemy is greed, not money, not power, and not people.

You need money and power as tools to perform your good medicine. This is another way of saying, you need money and power to carry out your good ideas and to be of benefit to humankind and all of our relatives. Now, let us get on with learning how to gather these tools and use them well toward our highest purposes.

"Medicine" as we are using the term herein means correction, healing, or bringing into balance. A shaman is a medicine person, one who tries to bring things into right relationship. It is extremely important that people of good medicine pick up the tools of power now and create a balanced world with them. You are the environmentally aware. You are the spiritually dedicated. You are the socially concerned. You are the healer, shaman, medicine person, business person that has come to make correction in the social fabric of our time.

The first step of a medicine person is to take notice of a distressing situation. I am going to assume that you are already well aware of more distress than you wish to think about. You realize at least one and perhaps hundreds of problems in the world. Some of them affect your life very personally. Some deeply trouble the people you care about most. Some are mild annoyances. Some are major catastrophes. Whatever you see, you see a need for change.

Your second step as a shaman is to make a commitment to use some of your particular talent or skill, some of your personal energy and resources, to move that distressing situation back into balance. A skillful shaman knows that even a little nudge might be enough to make a wave, to set up a vibration, that will cause healing to occur.

Your third step as you take up your medicine walk is to know your powers and how to use them. You will learn even more about your self than you already know as you do the exercises in this book. You will see that your talents need tools in order to interface with the world. Shaman's tools. You may be fascinated by magic wands, healing crystals, and mind power machines. It is interesting to study their effects. But "you ain't seen nothing" until you see the effect of money and business power on the world. In fact, you have seen it at its worst, because you have not been in charge.

Have all the doubts you want about wands and crystals, but you can have no doubt that money affects lives. Business affects people's every moment of their waking existence. For better or for worse, you have experienced it every day of your life. Money and business have taken the video camera into the deepest jungle to the most remote tribes. For better or worse. This is power.

In your hands this power and your money can do what you think is better. Shaman's tools. You need to be ready for them or they will use you. Worse than a dark crystal filled with a sorcerer's curse, your job, if you do not choose it and use it well, can eat up all of your life. Choose well the tools with which you will wield your power. Choose now to create some good.

Shaman's Tools 101

In business, your power comes from learning how to skillfully use the tools of your trade. You are used to thinking of items like the telephone, pens and paper, desks, and ledger books as ordinary non-magical things. But, as a medicine woman/man in business, you must begin to recognize them as shaman's tools. Consider the following.

The telephone is an instrument which gives you the power to move your thought thousands of miles. It conveys your emotion along with your message and allows you to receive the messages of others. It can be linked to a recording device which allows you to be in two places at once, your voice message staying at your desk while you go out. The answering machine can be used to check out your voice power, the subtle messages your voice tone projects to the listener, and it also gives you perfect recall of your client's requests. The answering machine can also be a shield protecting you from unwanted intrusions. Such a benefactor and guardian should be treated with respect.

You might want to put them in a special place or paint them in a way that reminds you of their real value in helping you achieve your goals. Who says they need to be brown? Maybe just a sticker symbolizing how you want to come across to your customers would remind you that you are using a shaman's tool when you answer the phone. If you want a better attitude toward being in business, you are going to have to do some things differently than you ever have before.

> *The discipline is called "being in business for yourself." It is no less holy, no less a part of the wholeness, than any traditional spiritual practice.*

Consider your desk. Is it a part of your kitchen table or is it more like a paper piling place? It could be an altar to Earth Mother, goddess of manifestation. Your desk is the place where the material realm is at your command, the command of a loving spiritual being. You come to this altar to practice a specific discipline. That discipline is the bringing forth into material reality the very highest of your spiritual heart's desires. The discipline is called "being in business for yourself." It is no less holy, no less a part of the wholeness, than any traditional spiritual practice.

You are a disciple of that God/Goddess which manifests as your talents, abilities, and qualities of being. At this altar, you give form to this godness and learn to extend your divine gifts to the world. Let your office become your power spot. Martial artists have a dojo in which to practice. The yogi has an ashram. Artists and dancers must have a studio. You, business shaman, must have your place to practice and perfect your art. It is your compassionate consciousness which must wield the tools of the powers that be in order to make a world in balance.

My Shaman's Tools

List your own business shaman's tools in this column.	List another way you could think of each one.
Example: telephone	voice teleporter

Spiritual Relationship

The technological culture tends to diminish the spiritual relationship you have to things. Advertising emphasizes emotional thrills from possessing something special, but only after you own that something do you realize that you must relate to it. It requires care, placement, upkeep, attention, perhaps the learning of new skills or the letting go of something old which it replaces. You must interact with every thing you possess.

Interaction, to be satisfying, must be a give and take relationship. If you think your telephone just interrupts you, your computer is irritating, your car takes all your money, and your house takes all your time, you are going to be unhappy. Unequal transactions - too much

13

giving, not enough receiving - are disruptive to your emotional equilibrium. These unbalanced relationships can be corrected, oftentimes, by simply renaming the items and the people that you are holding in negative thought.

The name or phrase you usually apply to something may be preventing you from seeing its true power in your life. The following is an example of renaming and rephrasing some everyday occurrences.

Each morning, an apprentice to the god Mercury gathers information from the elders you admire and people of your clan and brings messages, without disturbing you, to a small treasure box outside your door. Here, after your morning ritual, you retrieve these scrolls and retreat to your place of power before the altar of Your Highest Vision to consider them.

You give thanks that even though your treasure box is in plain sight, some kind of spell has been cast upon it which keeps anyone else from stealing its contents. Each day at a preordained time, the messenger comes. Each day, words of guidance appear. Now, as you sit in the chair no one else dare covet, you lean back to receive what has been written.

The letters are in secret code. The deciphering of them depends upon the knowledge which you have accumulated in your field, the many adventures that brought you to this high position. One scroll tells you of an ancient book of wisdom you may wish to procure and informs you of the feats of courage you must perform in order to win the honor of learning the secrets. The next scroll is from a distant pilgrim seeking to win your favor so that you will share your map to happiness. A third scroll encloses a magical green paper which can be transformed into anything you desire.

You set the scrolls aside now and look into your Book of Prophecy. Herein you have carefully inscribed figures in columns according to an alchemical formula which allows you to foresee the year ahead. Instantly, you know that this green paper substance just received is the final ingredient needed to turn a wish into reality. You close the Book of Prophecy and reach for your crystal telephone to project your thoughts. Your order is received.

You envision the pilgrim, wanting to share your wealth. Again, your communicating device is ready and waiting. Only a moment passes before you hear the pilgrim's voice. "I can help you," you say. With a few words, you weave a spell that is certain to bring her the wisdom she seeks.

You ponder the acts of power that must be made in the coming day. Travel. An interchange with a stranger. A search. Discovery of clues that might make your entire empire more secure. The possibility of surprise. You begin to get ready. With a prayer affirming your life pledge to reach the Ultimate Goal, you pack your shaman's tools. Dressed in full costume of your trade, you set out to conquer poverty, to overcome ignorance, to promote bliss. The day begins.

Now that's business! Every workday can be as magical as this when you relate to the spiritual aspect of each material form placed before you. The story reveals that the mail carrier has brought three letters, a promotional ad for a book, an order for something you offer, and a payment of a debt to you. Your cash flow journal predicts your financial future. It lets you know that you can purchase the book with the money received. You can help your customer because you continue to upgrade your knowledge by reading books applicable to your business. You know your target and you are willing to act.

Business terms such as "target" and "cash flow" may not mean much to you yet. But soon you will understand them and speak with authority translating your spiritual path into a means of right livelihood.

You begin being in business for yourself by noticing the needs of others. You do NOT start a business by deciding what you want to do. This is very important. You begin being in business for yourself by noticing the needs of others. Those others who need something are a "market." Your "target market" is those people with whom you might enjoy relating and who need something you might enjoy offering.
You MUST recognize your target market. Who are these people? Where do they live and work? How might you reach them?

Once you recognize your target market, you decide how you might fill their need. You find something they as a group need done and you decide to do it. You might use your own talents to fill the need or find others whom you will manage in order to get the need filled. Your target market becomes the tribe or community into which you have chosen to enter. You now dedicate yourself to serving them well.

Even if your "market" is the company which employs you, the same principles are at work. Your product becomes the work you were hired to do. You are selling it to your boss every day for an agreed upon price. If you want more money and the feeling of being in charge, read on. This book is for you as well as for those who want to actually start a new business themselves or improve the one they have begun.

Where once it was acceptable to wear certain feathers to symbolize your acts of power, now it is most appropriate to hand out your card as a statement of your courage to be who you are.

Once you have adopted the idea that you are in business for yourself, whether employee or entrepreneur, you can continue toward setting up the level of wealth and mastery you wish to attain. How to zero in on a market and decide on the product or service to offer will be discussed in later chapters. Meanwhile, let us continue our overview.

You have a targeted market. You have a product or service based on their need and your talents. Your tribe wants what you have to offer. You must now create the costume, chants, and symbols which will attract your tribe to the offerings you wish to place before them.

Business cards, stationery, and catalogs or brochures contain a powerful symbolic language called a logo. Your logo must speak volumes in a word or graphic image. Where once it was acceptable to wear certain feathers to symbolize your acts of power, now it is most appropriate to hand out your card as a statement of your courage to be who you are. Even your checks can say, "This is who I am. This is what I offer."

As you pass your card or currency from one hand to another, bless the transaction with goodwill. Offer the words which will open friendly communication, a chant of peace like, "May I be of service to you?"

Mean what you say. Do it to heal, to connect, to recognize someone as a member of the tribe you have chosen. You are forming a mutually supportive clan. It is called a network or a client group or simply, customers. Behave with integrity toward them.

You are casting a circle of business, a circle of wealth. Let everyone know her or his importance. Your wealth depends upon them. Their well-being depends upon you. Good business has a power to attract. Even if someone is very busy, you can attract their time and attention, their gifts and powers, if you offer to do business with them.

You can uplift their awareness once you have their attention if you treat your store or office like a Temple of Manifestation. It can be a place of fulfillment of their desires and yours. The more it is, the more successful you will be. Through your doors may come the lost, the hungry, the troubled, the confused, the lonely, the kind, the joyful, the proud, the silly, the saint. Depending on the symbols you have placed in public view, certain kinds of people will be called more than others. Yet surprises will always come too. Each one is a test or a treat for your spiritual consciousness.

All your powers will be called upon in business for yourself. It is an excellent medicine ground on which to become a spiritual warrior whose power restores balance to the world. Business is relationship. It is not only contracts and exchanges, but it is a proving ground for your spiritual point of view. Each person you contact can be met as though the divine dwells within.

Overcoming Obstacles

Even if you are presently dissatisfied with your financial or job situation, it is probably a somewhat comfortable dissatisfaction. You have accepted it, excused it, given it a good reason to exist. The reasons often heard for keeping things the way they are sometimes give certain objects or situations more power than they deserve. Look at the chart on the following page. See if you recognize any of your own phrases and the obstacles they protect.

If any of these sound familiar, make yourself a sign which says, "Obstacles give birth to creativity." Hang it where you will see it many times a day. Overcoming obstacles is the core of business. Being in business for yourself is all about inventing ways to solve problems, take shortcuts, find another way around, use the same old thing in a new

Obstacle Check-up

I hear myself saying:	Therefore, my obstacle appears to be:
"The children need me."	child care
"What if I fail?"	lack of basic security
"First I have to do the dishes."	household chore pile-up
"They just wouldn't stop talking."	"phone-y" friends
"Maybe I'll have a snack."	refrigerator too handy
"I couldn't put it down."	reading for escape
"When I get an office..."	present space too cramped
"Who would want what I do?"	entertaining self with puzzles
"I just couldn't say no."	accepting too many invitations
"But I never liked math."	fear of numbers, graphs, & charts
"I am no good at planning."	fear of losing spontaneity
"I hate paperwork."	fear of being overwhelmed
"I am not talented."	unwilling to look closely at what you have done thus far
"I don't know my purpose in life."	unable to set short-term goals
"No one would support this idea."	idea insufficiently developed
"When I get time..."	priorities not yet set

way, etc. Whatever your obstacle, let it be the first business problem you tackle successfully.

Put yourself in power. Right now, say out loud, "I am willing to change what I have been in order to become what I can be." You do not have to know the particulars yet. Just set your will on the right track. "I am willing to be in business for myself." With the will power willing, the magic begins. Everything you do from this point forward is going to help you know what your business is, who it serves, and why it is right for you.

You are no longer going to simply shuffle papers for a paycheck or sling tofu for tips. You are becoming an important person. It may start small, but you are going to control a financial empire all your own. This is a big buffalo hunt and you, as chief, are going to make sure the hunt happens in a holistic way. You are going to utilize every part of the sacred offering known as yourself to gather sustenance for your life. And you are going to gather enough to share with your whole tribe.

You are going to harness the power of money and use it for good. It is a warrior's task, a shaman's task. Your training is at hand. Every day you are going to accumulate power. If you have ever worked a job you hated, then you have been through your Vision Quest. You have deprived yourself of the best foods by not being able to afford them, sometimes given up the dearest friends by having to move away. You may have endured foul air and impure water, fought poverty and disease, suffered emotional distress under thoughtless bosses. You have passed the tests of self-denial separated from all who wish to support you. The quest ends now as you begin the powerful life, walking your medicine path through the world of being in business for yourself.

As you proceed, you will realize that the powers you gain will protect your children. Your knowledge, your values, your wealth will be passed on. This will happen because you have decided to be in the business which supports your true values in a way in which you can have time to be involved with your family in a place you want to live. You are putting yourself in a position to influence the future with the talents and skills that make up your being.

Even if your business is curling hair or changing tires, you are going to do it now as a medicine path. You are going to bring quality, beauty, kindness, fair trade, and clear contracts to your people. You are going to be an oasis of sanity and serenity in a chaotic time. You are going to savor the environment, making a home where your love can work, so that when you grow old you can say, "My love continues." Whether it is a village you have designed, a ring you have crafted, a book you have written, or a recipe for the very best bread, your work, your love, continues long after you have gone.

> *You were created with just the right talents and tendencies, offered just the right training and experiences, to do only one thing: to be yourself, fully and in today's world.*

It is a big job, but it is the only job that you were designed by G.O.D. (the Grand Overall Designer) to do. You were created with just the right talents and tendencies, offered just the right training and experiences, to do only one thing: to be yourself, fully and in today's world. That means, you are in business and you have what it takes.

Now, let us begin. There are twenty-two steps from taking the first foolish risk and trusting the hidden wonder within you to dancing on top of the world. These steps correlate with a deck of cards called the **Medicine Woman Tarot**. The cards provide images for the ideas herein, but you may easily supply your own instead. I recommend that you take a photo of yourself to symbolize every step of the way. Keep a journal of your progress.

Going into business for yourself, even if it is only changing the way you think about being an employee, is serious, life-changing, fun, and an experience you will want to share with your grandchildren. After all, you will be saving and replenishing the Earth for them. You may want to show them some "before" pictures.

Go through the lessons, Zero to Twenty-One, one at a time. Take as long as you need. This is not a "get rich quick" book, but it is a "find true happiness" book. So do not hurry through the good parts. Enjoy your life. Is this not the reason you wish to make your change?

My Obstacles Give Birth to My Creativity

My obstacles appear to be:	My creative response is:

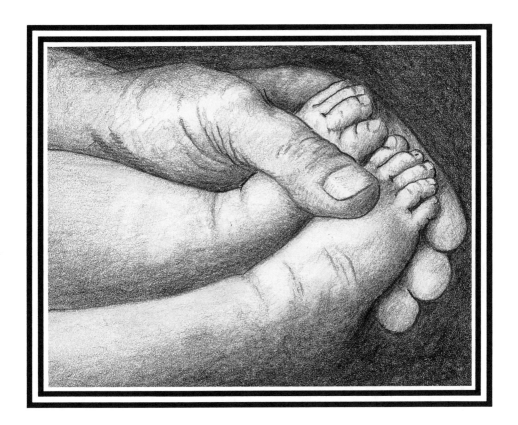

The Seed

Every idea starts from nothing, the emptiness within the center of the circle, the zero, the void, the hole in your personal universe. Out of the infinite field of wonder, emerging from deep blue peace comes an image which inspires. At this point, some people feel they have it, the key to success. Now they are going to be rich, famous, all troubles dissolved. Then they begin their list of "if onlys," obstacles such as those listed in the previous chapter.

The vision comes. The vision is obstructed. The idea remains a zero, a seed unplanted. In the world of nature, many seeds are given so that a few are sure to take root. Many seed ideas are offered to the minds of those dreaming and imagining, so that each idea may find the fertile soil of willingness in someone ready to bring forth the new.

I am assuming that you want to capture the seed, to nurture the new idea within yourself, to move past obstacles and on to the fulfillment of the vision which has or will come to you. I believe you want to work in a meaningful occupation while you pursue your spiritual quest, fulfilling your desires for a life richly endowed with the treasures of transcendent experience. I am also assuming that you have bills to pay, maybe a mortgage, rent, tuition, car expenses, perhaps loans, and the responsibilities of caring for a family. If you will follow lessons zero through twenty-two increasing your awareness of the powers of the four directions, you will see how seemingly oppressive obligations can be changed into benefactors.

Accomplishment Zero - Receive the Seed

Your dream of the good life for yourself may have already been with you a long time, perhaps since childhood. If so, it is time to look at it again. You have grown, some things have changed. Perhaps there are parts of it you do not really want anymore. Or, you may have lost your childhood dream and be ready for a new vision. Either way, the first thing I am going to suggest is that you go into a relaxed and receptive state so that a seed idea can be given.

Shut the door. Turn off your connections to the outside world, such as the television and the telephone. Situate yourself in a comfortable chair. Fifteen minutes is all you need right now. This is your Seed Break. Loosen tight clothing or shoes. Stretch. Breathe deeply. And relax. Sit back and begin to imagine your perfect life. No holds barred. No age, money, or other limitations. No rational thought about it. Just daydreaming the seemingly impossible. The way you like it. Put the book down now and really do this for fifteen minutes.

Did you get a picture? If not, do not worry. Sometimes people cannot let themselves have a great life even in their imagination. They may feel inhibited by guilt or unworthiness. If this is your situation, think of someone else who is living a life you admire. Perhaps with a few exceptions or embellishments, it could be the life for you. Close your eyes again and put yourself in the picture. Make any adjustments necessary for your total comfort with their lifestyle. How rich are you? How generous? How tranquil? How much time do you spend in nature? What kind of activities do you enjoy most? Who is with you? How often are they with you? What part of the country is home? What are the spiritual rewards from living this lifestyle?

> *This is ground zero, the beginning, the circle of openness, of possibility, of nothing set, nothing formed. All is yet to come into actual being.*

Just meander and play in and out of the possibilities in your imagination. This is ground zero, the beginning, the circle of openness, of possibility, of nothing set, nothing formed. All is yet to come into actual being. Get the idea? Seeds are falling from the hands of Creator. Catch a few. What kind of flower are you? Play with all the possibilities for one may become an opportunity. But no decisions today. Nothing to worry about. No need to choose yet. No need to commit. Let them all return to zero.

That may be all you have time for right now. If so, that is enough. Go back to your daily work and pick this book up again whenever you have time for the next step, which we will call Accomplishment One because this was Accomplishment Zero. Remember, zero is a necessary place to be. Until you are ready for Accomplishment One, be open to external images, such as magazine photos, paintings, or real life scenes which resemble your inner Seed Images of the life you might want to be living in the surroundings in which you might want to live it. If possible, collect those images in a folder or describe them in a notebook for use in a later exercise.

This brings us to Important Success Tool #0, the blank book. If you do not have one, buy one now. Get one that "feels like you," the you of your imagining.

Review - Accomplishment Zero

Zero - Be nothing. Be empty. Be open.
Seed - Become aware of the seed of your personal paradise within.
Gather - Find pictures which depict the life you might want to live.
Plant - Look at them every chance you get.
Buy Important Success Tool #0 - a notebook. And get ready to begin filling in the unknown.

First Impressions

My Land

My Building

My Career

How I Dress

People With Me

How I Travel

What I Eat

My Entertainments

My Inspiration

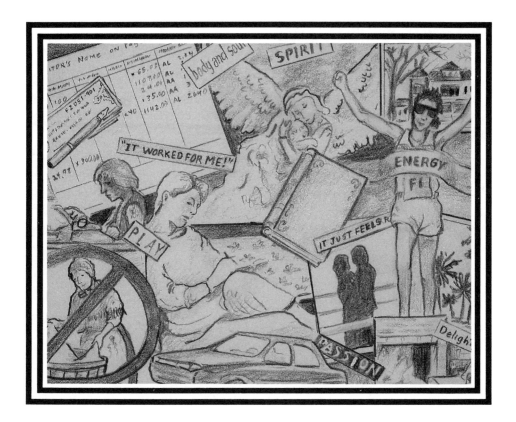

Resources

The first step in manifesting the life you desire or even to bring about anything close to a life you might enjoy is to embrace the seed and give it your resources. I have not asked you to look critically at the Seed Images you have collected. This was not an accidental omission. You need to take a few other steps first while the dream is still fresh and full of life. I know you might be thinking, "No way can I afford this fantasy!" But hold on.

Embrace the Seed. Put those pictures you have collected on the wall where you can see them often, preferably in front of where you work or make decisions. Above them make a sign which says, "Does it get me closer to this?" That will give you immediate feedback when

31

you are making small daily choices. You will know whether you are going in the direction of your "best life" fantasy or not. As far as possible make even the smallest decisions in support of this "best life" direction.

Once again, do not try to decide ahead of time whether, in fact, it IS the best life. Just trust the Seed Images and go toward them. As you go toward them, it will either feel very good or terrible. If it feels terrible, think about it. Is there something you actually prefer more? Reconstruct your Seed Image; add or subtract a piece of the picture according to your newfound desire. The small choices and the acting upon them are your best homing devices. Keep shifting your Seed Images according to your ACTUAL EXPERIENCE, not preconceived ideas about what you SHOULD enjoy or how you OUGHT to live.

Accomplishment One - Acknowledge Resources

Again looking over your Seed Images, what are the resources shown?

Land - What kind? Forest, hills, farm, seacoast? How much? Acres? a secluded spot? A city lot? Where? Close to what? Anywhere that has this kind of terrain? Far from something in particular?

Building - What would be the general description of your living quarters? How close to other dwellings, to friends? Of what materials is the building constructed?

Career - What do you see yourself doing, ideally, that makes it all possible? How is it you enjoy spending time? (Remember, you are still musing, not choosing.)

Clothing - How do you dress day to day, on the job, off the job?

People - Who is with you? What is your relationship with those who share your life?

Means of Transportation - Do you have a truck, a car, a plane, a pony? Is walking your joy?

Food - Where do you dine and what do you eat? Get a picture that shows the feeling at your table.

Things - What do you enjoy tinkering with? How are you entertained? What relaxes you, inspires you?

All creation begins in imagination, but it does not stay there.

Keep collecting those magazine images. Madison Avenue has spent millions of dollars giving you high class full color glossies. You might as well use them to inspire you toward what you REALLY want. If you notice something in the pictures you do not like, cut it off, cross it out, or cover it up. Replace it with some missing piece you just realized you need instead. When your picture collage is complete in a general sense, you should be able to look at it and feel, "Ah, yes, this is the life for me." Rearrange it until you can. Then stick a photo of yourself right in the middle as a message to your subconscious to "Take me here."

Then get out your blank notebook and begin, in your own special way, to list all of the parts of the Seed Vision you already have. You may have a 50' x 100' plot of suburban lawn when you desire 40 acres of mountaintop. Still, you must realize, "This is land, my first portion of the land which is coming to me; and I am going to treat it like my mountaintop." Maybe you have a one-bedroom apartment in the city when you long for an oceanside cottage. Write down, "I have three of the rooms of my future cottage. Where my window would look out upon the sea, I am hanging my favorite seascape to remind me of the place I will someday be."

If all of this is beginning to sound too esoteric, be assured that it is only Accomplishment One of twenty-two accomplishments you will be achieving. All creation begins in imagination, but it does not stay there.

Continue to list the parts of your Seed Vision which you now have. Include skills that will come in handy in your future potential career. Recognize that you have some of the clothes, the food, and the things that you will keep in your future lifestyle. The more you can list, the better you will feel. You may also have some of the friends you hope will be around to enjoy this future with you. Really take stock. Walk around your house, yard, and office making this list. Check off, "Yes, I would keep that." "No, that has to go." And get rid of everything that will not take the trip with you. As soon as you can! Everything. Off to Goodwill, someone who needs it, the recycling center, or wherever it will do the most good. Things were meant to serve, not to sit. If it is not a part of your future, keep it only if it is an item of devotion, your altar honoring your past. Do not keep dead weight.

Of course you are going to discover a few things you love but which will not last long and a few things you hate but which will have to accompany you for awhile. Consider these temporary "employees." Write down their expected last day of employment and the item which is going to replace them when they are retired.

As you can see, there is beginning to be a need for record keeping and planning. Several lists may be happening, "What I Have," "What to Get Rid Of," "To Goodwill," "To Mom," "To the Dump," etc. Do not freak out. This frustration with keeping track of everything is letting you know the importance of Success Tool #1, the calendar. Go get one now with big spaces for each day. Come back to this book and your next Accomplishment, The Seeker, after you have made your lists and written on your calendar the dates of WHEN you are going to accomplish your giveaways. Look at it this way, once all that stuff is gone, it will be quite a bit easier to see the real resources you have, love, and want to take with you.

Review - Accomplishment One

One - Look at yourself, the one in the center of your Seed Images, the one in the center of your future.

Resources - Notice that you already have many parts of the whole of your future. Give away excess baggage.

List - what stays, what goes.

Important Success Tool #1 - a calendar. Buy one and make this the year for YOU.

To tithe is to give away 10% of your talents to your people - offer them free - and to allow all unused belongings to be passed on to where they can again become useful.

Seeker

You may have unearthed some feelings as you looked over the pictured future and the past as it stood symbolized by your belongings. These feelings are real. They are valid. These may be the emotions you shelved when you were too busy in that life you are leaving behind. You are leaving your old life behind, you know, at least parts of it, the parts you do not want to carry anymore.

Anytime you lay down a burden, there is a release of energy which occurs. It may bring tears of sadness or joy. The burden was, after all, something which accompanied you like a friend. It served a purpose. It may have played an important role in your life. You may not wish to see it as a burden, just something which is completed. Either way, honor it with thanks for the part it played. And let it go. Pass it on. Free it for a new life.

Accomplishment Two - Seek the Undiscovered Self

You are travelling now. Travel light. To get to your new territory, you must leave the old. You have reviewed what can travel with you and what cannot. Make your peace. Look back with love. And say, "Good-bye."

> *Anytime you lay down a burden, there is a release of energy which occurs.*

Depending upon your situation, you may be parting from poverty or leaving a memory. Work with these inner partings now as only you can. Take time. This is what your new life offers, time to recognize what was good about the past, to feel, to know, to enjoy and to suffer good-byes. My only advice at this step is, do not leave your job, get a divorce, or move from your physical home at this time. Such important life changes should not come at step two. The Seeker stage is the phase of looking within, of feeling first and giving those feelings time to bring wisdom.

If you did not bring up memories and emotions as you took stock of your resources, go back and do a more thorough job this time. Remember how you acquired all those things, what it took, how you had to grow, who helped you. Take your time, take days if you need them. You are making a clear place for the energy of your Seed to push through.

Making room stirs things up. The seed within you stirs and wonders if and where and how it will grow. You are helping it to break ground, to seek its potential, to imagine its yet undiscovered self. Just know that these whirls of feeling arising are natural at this point in the process. You are not just reading a book, you are actually making a major life shift.

Review - Accomplishment Two

Two - Look at your relationship to everything you have. Life review is the "me and you" of relationship.
Seeker - Feel the stirring. Seek the light. Prepare to let go of all that cannot fit into your future.
Important Success Tool #2 - Two eyes for crying. Two eyes to see. Use them.

I Cry and I See

Right now, I feel like crying about

Bounty

With eyes dry and a fresh start, get out your calendar and notebook. For everything listed in your notebook as a "must go," schedule the day of its departure on your calendar. Be real. It took you years to accumulate this stuff. It is not all leaving this week. Your calendar is blank. Consider this the Great Spirit's way of saying, "You have 365 free days this year; what are you going to do with them?"

Accomplishment Three - Experience Bounty

The first experience of Bounty can be the bounty of time. You

41

may have already made plans for 350 of those days just by being a parent or a student or an employee; but there is still time. You have time to reconsider...not whether to parent, go to school, or work...but how and how often you will be actively involved in these enterprises. Right now, act as if all 365 days were empty and free. Then pick several days scattered over the course of the year when you will indeed drop off your past, your unwanted old items. Each appointment thus created is an appointment with freedom, with space, with new energy, health and vitality.

> *Consider this the Great Spirit's way of saying, "You have 365 free days this year; what are you going to do with them?"*

Except for the "biggies" of primary relationship commitment, present job responsibilities, and any desire for a change of location, your life is now "cleaned up." You are scheduled to rid yourself of all distractions and obstacles to your good life within the year. If you are lucky, your present significant other is someone you love, your job is at least preparing you for some part of your new career, and you live in a place that, with a few improvements, would not be bad at all. If so, pause; count your blessings.

If you are not so lucky in regard to spouse, house, and employment, do not fear. This book deals with it all. For now, however, write in your notebook the first "biggie" that you are going to have to tackle. Prioritize if there is more than one. Then give yourself a date by which you will have given all you are willing to give to this person, job, or place; in other words, decide on an end time for your relationship to her, him, or it. Write it on your calendar. That will be it. No extensions. No emotional juice after this date.

Until then, you are saying to yourself, "I will do what I know I can do well to make whatever arrangements are needed so that this will be a pleasant ending." You know what you are capable of doing. You may feel that you have already "tried your best" to make the relationship work; you may have "given it all you've got." Good. Now, bring your talents, compassion, and creativity to bear on making a beautiful ending. Tie up loose ends. Do what brings you a sense of emotional completion. But stop letting this "trying" be open-ended. The date is set. Stick to it.

The coming year will not be the easiest one you have ever lived, but it may be the most significant. It can be the opening to the bountiful gifts of life that you never thought you could have. Are you willing to put in one year of work toward the future which holds your heartfelt dreams? I think you are.

Review - Accomplishment Three

Three - Make your appointments with Freedom. Start packing that old stuff out.
Bounty - Count your blessings, especially time and the will to take charge.
Important Success Tool #3 - A bounty of three treats: give yourself three things you seldom allow yourself to have.

My Three Treats

1.	
2.	
3.	

Command

The feelings of emerging personal power should by now be welling up inside you. You are taking command of who you are, what you do, where you live. This is a huge Earth-healing step. Consider the idea that it is very unecological to have one human being, much less, millions of them, running around on the planet using up resources doing boring, loveless, uncreative work. True, there are worse disasters, but how much more healing to the planet Earth to have her beings filled with exuberance for carrying out the work for which their talents have prepared them. An uninspired human is a waste of energy.

With the current state of the planet, all human creative energy is needed to bring a new and harmonious order to civilization. If we do not, we will all be fired. The business called Earth will fold. And if you have been worried about losing your present job security in order to risk a new life, dwell for a minute on the alternative of slowly experiencing the loss of clear water, fresh air, healthful food, the means to shelter, and as a result, the loss of a well family, frisky pets, the song of birds in the morning, flowers in the spring. Life as we have known it is severely threatened. Right now. We cannot afford to hang out on this planet being one of the needy, a body of wasted talents and dead emotions. Earth is a place of beauty by nature and can support a diversity of cultures who enhance her beauty if we care for her.

Look at your Seed Images. Do they not contain Earth's beauty? Are not the places you wish to live and work the "protected" areas, where life still thrives? These are becoming fewer and fewer. Sadly, in my own lifetime, I have never observed an improvement of Earth's environment on any large scale other than the short-lived renaissance of small town and old building renovation of the early 1970's. Mainly, I have witnessed the cementing over of nature's bounty. Yet, I know you are still there, as individuals, doing what you can under the circumstances of your situation.

Accomplishment Four - Take Command

In spite of this predicament - lack of support, lack of money, lack of models, lack of time, energy, or whatever restrictions have come down upon us - I believe I am supposed to be here, alive and working. I think that you, too, have made the choice to keep on living, that even as bad as it gets sometimes, you do want to be here. Perhaps you feel some Greater Power is keeping you alive for a reason. I think you will know more clearly what that reason is as you take command.

Consider yourself employed by The Goddess. (Substitute your own word for the Great All That Is, please; do not be limited by mine.) You have been hired by the Grand Overall Designer, G.O.D. as she is sometimes called, and stationed in a particular place and time. You have already put in several years at the lower levels of this job developing your skills and discovering some of your talents and things you love doing. Now, you are up for promotion.

Today, you are becoming Manager of Your Own Territory. Admittedly, the territory might be small when you compare it to the whole Earth, but it is an integral part of G.O.D.'s company. If you do a good job here, well, who knows what the Boss Lady might offer you next? Now that she can see your goals (the Seed Images over your desk), at least she knows what you have in mind. She can see that you want to be upwardly mobile in a new sense of the term, that you want a position in keeping with your higher consciousness.

If you can't keep your room clean, how do you expect to clean up the planet?

There was a time when you were willing to take any assignment. The Goddess tested your capabilities under certain family and social conditions, school and health challenges, and some work in the larger world. You did the best you could. Now you think you can do a good job in a specific area of your own choice. You have some new ideas based on your experience and education, and you would like a chance to try them out. You have your notebook and calendar. You are clearing away distractions and making space for the new you, designing the office and the territory. She has to notice.

You have cleaned your room or your whole house (Haven't you?). You have begun to order your small world the same way that you would like to order the big world. (If you can't keep your room clean, how do you expect to clean up the planet?) If you have not completed these steps, put the book down and TAKE COMMAND. This is the task at hand. When complete, read on.

It is time for Important Success Tool #4, your new title. Try some of these to see how they fit you:

(Your Name), Manager of _(Your Address)_
            Manager of _(Your Talents)_
            Secret Earth Ecology Agent of (Your Present Employer)

Office Harmonizer of _(Your Present Workplace)_
Security Manager for _(Your Family)_
Developer of _(Your Future Business)_
President of _(Your New Business)_
Scholar of _(Your Major Interest)_
Regional Expert in _(Your Skill)_
Chief Executive Officer of _(Yourself)_
Founder of (Name of Charitable Work You Do)
Keeper of the Beauty of _(Your Land)_
Creator of _(Your Art)_

Be creative. Find the words that feel best to you, a description by which you would enjoy being recognized. The title may seem grandiose at the moment, but you will grow into it. The point is that you must accept a role of authority because you are becoming the author of your own life.

You have already carried a good deal of responsibility without getting credit for what you have done. A title is recognition. You must recognize yourself before others can recognize and respect you.

If you want to go all the way with this exercise, I recommend going to an office supply store and either buying a plaque or having a certificate made which entitles you. You may have a friend skilled in calligraphy to do this for you.

If you are already at the stage of your life where you are presently starting your own business, your title is even more important. You will be putting it on brochures or contracts and numerous other business forms. The public must find you believable in your titled role. In other words, you do not want them to laugh or to think that you are not capable of living up to your title. You must title yourself at the highest expression of the expertise you have achieved, but no higher than you are willing to attempt to be.

Some of the suggested titles are definitely inappropriate for serious business with the public, but they are serious steps for someone not yet in the public eye. If you cannot manage your room, for instance, you cannot manage an office or a business. Start where you are and become adept there. Make a title appropriate to your circumstances.

If you think you can run your own business, but your private affairs are a shambles, you are very mistaken. Stop now to reconsider. You may be an excellent employee due to a highly developed skill while you are messy at home, but you will never make it as a manager. Save yourself grief and accept your present limitations. Being in business for yourself successfully requires competent, ever-vigilant management. This is a skill you can develop by starting at home, in your room, in your self. Choose the title befitting you now. Better to manage your home and garden well than to poorly conduct the affairs of several employees and waste company (Earth's) resources.

There once was a time when one, especially if you were male, could focus on business in the world while your partner, usually your wife, focused on keeping up the home. That time is almost gone as two jobs are required to pay the bills or to afford the frills. But, if you can arrange a setup where an associate handles all areas where you are less competent and he or she is skilled, go ahead. Nice work if you can get it. The important thing in such an arrangement is that each of you KNOW YOUR ROLE and take command in your own area. In this case, you should each have an appropriate title which encompasses the real work you do. "Wife" does not cover it. Nor does "husband."

More will be said on clear contracts with others in later chapters. For now, it is simply time to give yourself permission to take command of that portion of your life you feel yourself capable of stewarding. It is an important job at every level. Do not jump ahead of where you are ready to be. Each position carries responsibilities as well as self-esteem and public recognition.

You are casting a spell, "spell"ing words to define yourself. The words should create a structure in which you can grow toward full expression of your highest potential. The title defines your new area of authority, that which your are willing to take command of now. If you do a good job here, you will find self-promotion easy. I know there is an area in which, with proper recognition, you can excel. Now, go define it.

Review - Accomplishment Four

Four - Create a title which defines your present area of authority and which allows you to increase your expertise. This is a foundation structure upon which you shall build your future.

Command - Look at your life and the home/work environment around you from the perspective of being the manager.

Important Success Tool #4 - A title. Four words or fewer work best.

My Title

Peacemaker

You have given yourself the task of authority over a certain area of life. Whether it is small or large, you must now make peace with it. Walk around. Get to know your space: your room, your home, your land, your office, your neighborhood, the places your life touches. If you were in charge, how would you bring peace here? What calls out to you? What would you change? Where are you comfortable? Where do you feel in command? This is your territory. Walk the terrain with your new title in mind. How does it feel? Imagine that this is all yours. You are now entitled to it. Let it sink in.

It is here that you are going to interface with the world. You are going to meet people, exchange with them, retreat here. What do you need in order to make that easy and pleasant? This is the portion of the world to which you have become entitled. Your title designates you as authority of this area or a portion thereof. You are assuming command of a new function. Imagine what it might be like.

Accomplishment Five - Make Space for Peace

A manager must have space for interfacing with others and a space for being alone. And there will be many spaces or times when others will reside with you or pass through your space. You must begin to make the boundaries clear. When and where will each kind of activity happen?

> *You must have a personal, private oasis where nothing interferes. If you must begin with a space as small as a basket or a medicine bag like your briefcase, so be it. It is yours and it is sacred.*

First, let us create your own private space where no one is ever allowed to go without invitation. It may be your studio, your desk, your altar, your secret place in the woods. Wherever it is, let others know, in words they can peacefully accept, that this space is off limits. Your private space is an office where you and G.O.D. decide on courses of action. It is a place where you and The Goddess share a very personal love. It is a peacemaker itself, for it makes peace in you.

You must have a personal, private oasis where nothing interferes. If you must begin with a space as small as a basket or a medicine bag like your briefcase, so be it. It is yours and it is sacred.

For simplicity, I am going to assume you have a room. Now, in that room, begin to develop a sense of reverence. Here is where your relationship to the invisible begins. Although you can see physical walls and furnishings, the space is also air and energy and vibrations. It is silence and feelings and prayers. It consists of wonderings and wishes and secret joys and sorrows untouched by the voices of others. Your space is emptiness, the place of emptying into the void. It is the zero, the beginning, the container of the Seed. Your space is the cup which will be filled by your love. Your space is time with the Infinite. The more you recognize these things, the more the space will nourish you.

You will start to love your space, to feel at home there, at peace, at one with everything around you. It will be your foundation of harmony, your source of creativity. The more it is respected, the more life it will seem to have. No matter how small it is, it will draw great power to you within it. You will emerge from your space to enter the world with confidence. Having touched your space, you will face challenges with equanimity. Having received the blessings of private moments of renewal, you will go out health-filled. Having interacted with all of your skill and talent with your space, you will know who you truly are. You will present this self to the world. And you will make peace.

Review - Accomplishment Five

Five - Four walls plus you make a space you can rule.
Peacemaker - Make a space which is totally nourishing to yourself. Make all of the boundaries clear in a peaceful way.
Important Success Tool #5 - Your private "office."

Sketch of My Personal Oasis

I have authority over:

I can make this area better by:

Other people would enjoy meeting me here if:

I make it clear when I want no one around by:

Ecstasy

With your Seed Ideas clear, obstacles of the past scheduled for removal, present resources in sight, a new title, a private oasis, and your emotional body cleansed with fresh tears and perked up by three treats, take a day off to enjoy the new stage you have set for yourself.

Accomplishment Six - Invite Ecstasy

You may want to invite a close companion over to reflect with you upon your changes. If so, be sure it is someone who will totally approve of the new you. Allow yourself, perhaps with the aid of your friend, to explore the positive ramifications of what you have just done. Think of how your Seed actions might benefit others you meet and care about. Imagine the good feelings, health, and self-confidence you will acquire as you pursue the path of living depicted in your Seed Ideas.

This is not a day for doubts or fears, but a day to indulge in the utmost positive thinking. Become your new life today. Act it out in all its glory. You need the physical experience of this day of ecstasy in your memory storehouse. Later, it will serve as a reminder of why you are doing what you are doing. It will also remind you of how your customers or clients want to feel as they do business with you.

> *You need the physical experience of this day of ecstasy in your memory storehouse. Later, it will serve as a reminder of why you are doing what you are doing.*

Celebrate in the mode that your new lifestyle - your Seed Ideas - suggests. With your house now arranged to your liking, surround yourself with objects which speak to you of comfort, success, and luxury as you define these qualities. Notice the sounds, the textures, the smells you enjoy most. This is your day. A new beginning. Let the mood be festive, tranquil or sacred, as you prefer. Set the tone for your new life. Acknowledge that you are entering a realm of Great Mystery. You are embarking on a mission to fulfill a dream. You are following your highest inspiration. You are consciously, bravely stepping into the Unknown with everything you are.

You are becoming a dynamic force for good. You are drawing to yourself universal energies with which you are going to weave a whole new life. Look at your Seed Ideas. Forming this collage is like drawing in color and fine detail. Drawing is the art of pulling forth energies, things, and people into pleasing combination. You are now becoming an artist who chooses those energies, things, and people herself and who creates the blend which fully expresses your style.

In the broadest sense, you are going into the business of making love. You are learning to create love with every action you perform in every place you go. Today, do what you love the way you love to do it. Do anything you <u>must</u> do with a style of your own. Bring your self-expression to even the most mundane tasks. Love the way you do them.

Though all parts of your life may not yet be deemed love-worthy, do what you can this day to love how you deal with them. Let those things you cannot yet change simply be as they are, as much as possible, letting them flow right on by without disturbing your comfort. This is the day of rest, the day of personal pleasures, the time of pleasing the person you really are.

Review - Accomplishment Six

Six - Think of six positive pleasures. Participate in as many as possible today.
Ecstasy - Enjoy the way you make art of your life.
Important Success Tool #6 - The scheduled day of rest.

My Positive Experience Day is scheduled for:

I am going to invite:

Warrior

If you have come this far, the worst is behind you. Inertia has been your worst enemy. Just to buy a new notebook may have been a major step. Then, you had to take an inventory of your whole life, all your stuff, your relationships, make decisions, plan to get rid of handicaps and actually schedule it all into your life. Next, you were left in control of some unruly space with boundaries you had to decipher and order you had to create. Not only that, you were put through the gamut of emotions in the process. All this for a promotion. And where is the increase in pay?

Here it comes. Not only are you organizing your life, but you are going to become a financial warrior as well. It is time for Important

Success Tool #8, the financial ledger. Go to the office supply store and buy one of those green 12 column ledger notebooks and a three column ledger notebook too. All of those straight lines are going to guide you to riches. Think of it as being like driving on your side of the road; you will not get to your destination if you do not stay within the lines. These lines and the numbers within them are your road map to success.

Accomplishment Seven - Become a Financial Warrior

I am going to assume that you are now in your private oasis, protected somehow from the world of distractions. You have your Seed Ideas clearly before you, your calendar and notebook nearby, and feel comfortable in your new titled position. If your private space is too small to be "within," then it is nearby and you are at least alone for the time being.

Now gather all of the information you need to inform you of your financial obligations. Your list may include, but is not limited to, the following: rent, utilities, food, car, health care, clothing, books, etc.

List, on the following page or in your three column notebook, all of the items you presently pay or should be paying toward each month. Then list the items for which you would like to save.

Be sure to include anything your Seed Ideas require which you do not already have. On the Financial Obligations page, fill in the items on which you owe money, the amounts of each monthly expense and the date each bill is due. If some are due quarterly or weekly, translate that into a monthly requirement. On the Things I Am Saving For page, fill in the items you desire, their cost and the date by which you would like to have all of these things. Also write in anything you want within this year on your calendar, scheduling the date you plan to get it.

You may need to do some calling to find out how much certain items you want will cost. On your calendar, schedule when you will make these calls. Fill in your ledger with all of the amounts as soon

Financial Obligations

Obligation/Debt	Monthly Expense	Date Due

Things I Am Saving For

Thing Or Event	Cost	Desired By (Date)

as you have the information. Some costs may have to be estimates. Be as accurate as possible. Gather the information you need to be in the know. Total Financial Obligations and Things You Are Saving For.

On another page, list your Income Sources and arrive at a monthly total. If you have a small or temporary shortage of funds, consider what items can be reduced by how much or postponed for how long. Call those creditors (the people to whom you owe money) and arrange your payment plan with them. Schedule this on your calendar. I know you do not want to make these calls, but this is Accomplishment Seven, the Warrior. Simply say, "This is when I <u>can</u> pay you." Then be sure you do so.

If you are seriously short of money to meet your monthly obligations, you must change your situation fast. Here are your options:

* Get a very short term job with the highest pay and the most hours, doing anything you can handle. It will not be your life's work.
* Sell something. Have a garage sale. Sell your VCR, your paintings, your services.
* Go for a walk through town. Every time you see something broken, dirty windows, grass too long, garbage strewn, paint peeling, stop to see if someone will pay you to fix it.
* Move to a cheaper location now...unless you are living in your ideal homestead which you have been paying on for 29 years until you lost your job. If that is the case, sell everything else instead.

Avoid getting loans, writing resumes, reading the want ads over coffee, and calling your friends. Take your samurai sword and slice off the offending debt fast. This is war.

And about going back to school, do not. I have often seen the financially desperate and those confused about their life work decide to go back to finish the degree program they dropped out of because they hated it or to study some new interesting subject which may never relate to the career they have not yet decided upon. Although with a tuition grant, returning to college could relieve some pressure, going back to school on deferred payment loans when your future is still

Income Sources

Source	Amount Due	Date Due

unclear is digging a hole out of which you will struggle to climb for years.

Go to school only to learn something clearly related to your Seed Ideas which you cannot learn any other way. Go only long enough to learn that thing. If you just need a degree behind your name in order to fulfill your life plan, there are more creative ways to get it than sitting in classes acquiring debts. Consider External Degree Programs or Self-Acquired Competency Tests. Adult Education classes or finding a tutor in your specific area and becoming an apprentice to a master are other ways to more quickly gather the specific knowledge you need at much less financial cost and time expenditure.

> *Your ledger books will soon become like Guardian Angels protecting you from financial disaster, prophesying when those good things you desire shall come to you.*

If yours is the dire situation of immediate need for money just to survive this month, stop reading now and go get it. Do not stop looking for the way to earn the immediate money you need until you have explored all of the options listed and one of them has worked. Consider this a full time job until you have found employment. Work this temporary job only until you are once again solvent. Then come back to this book.

Let us assume now that you have this month under control financially, and you foresee that next month will be much the same. Look again at your Monthly Income Total. Compare it to your Total Financial Obligations and Things I Am Saving For. If you have a large amount of excess income - these days it is called "discretionary" or "disposable" - just grant each of your items listed under Financial Obligations and Things I Am Saving For a portion of it, and your budgeting is complete. If you have some discretionary income, but not enough to easily cover all the things you want to do with it, here is what to do.

First, apportion all income needed for your Financial Obligations and prioritize from most to least important. Give yourself a total dollar amount available for saving each month this year. Now, prioritize your Things I Am Saving For. Then apportion part of that amount to each of the items in the column. Do not worry about how small and seemingly ridiculous the amount might be.

Even if you are putting 50 cents a month toward your Retirement and $5 toward A Car That Runs, you are making headway. You may be tempted to calculate how long it will take you to reach the cost of each item, but this can be depressing. At this time, it is not the point. The point is learning to budget and plan and to carry out these plans. You are becoming a warrior. The warrior gives her all no matter what.

Open savings accounts for the large amounts you will be putting aside, one for each item. Use piggy banks for the small amounts. Do not take this money out of the banks for any reason but its designated purpose. That would be like letting the air out of your tires every 50 miles. You have to take a journey. You are in the seventh phase of the trip. You are off to a good start. Keep going.

Your income will increase as you proceed through these exercises, and more and more you will be doing what you love. Keep scheduling what must be done on your calendar - when to go to the bank to open those accounts. Keep noting ideas generated from your Seed Ideas in your notebook. Continue ordering your space. Take time to peacefully experience the emotion of life as it flows through you. Things are shifting now, subtle changes are taking place. You are becoming a warrior, fiercely fighting to clear the path to your dreams.

Your ledger books will soon become like Guardian Angels protecting you from financial disaster, prophesying when those good things you desire shall come to you.

Review - Accomplishment Seven

Seven - Success comes from creating the order.
Warrior - Make financial change by taking charge and balancing your accounts.
Important Success Tool #7 - The financial ledger.

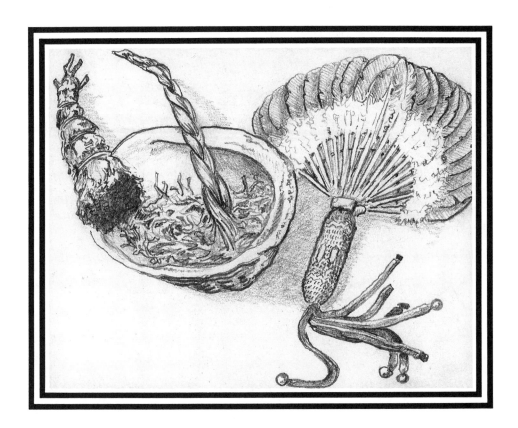

Healing

It is now time to tackle one of the "biggies." Take a quick mental inventory of the following: your major relationship, your present job, your present home, the current state of your health, how you feel about your friends, the state of your family affairs, the reputation you hold in the community you feel yourself to be a part of, and where you are in relation to your spiritual tradition.

On the following page is a quick exercise to assist you. Fill in the outlines or doodle around them quickly depicting the state of affairs in each of these areas. This is a shorthand way of letting yourself know what is going on. Wherever things are out of harmony with your Seed Ideas, choose from the options listed (or others you may create) and

69

Doodles

plan your course of repair.

Relationship
☐ Schedule a time out to talk things over. Share the fondness you really feel.
☐ Arrange for professional counselling.
☐ Discuss the best plan for parting, including when and how.

Present Job
☐ Consider whether you can be in the business of managing your life toward the manifestation of your Seed Ideas while working in your present position.
☐ Decide how long you are going to need your present position. It may be temporary until a certain amount of savings is reached in your Business Start-Up Fund account. It may be temporary until a certain skill is acquired or a level of expertise reached. Or it may be a job you can grow with for the rest of your life if you realize the command you can have within the situation.
☐ All but the latter can be scheduled on your calendar. If your "graduation" to a new level is beyond one year from now, just make a note of when it is coming at the end of your calendar.

Present Home
☐ How long will it suit your purposes? Schedule when it needs to change.
☐ Look it over carefully. Could it be remodeled to suit your future?
☐ If you are renting and hope to someday own, be sure you have opened your "Future Home" savings account.
☐ Schedule in any repairs or changes you can afford this year.

Personal Health
☐ Schedule your Well Days Off for the year.
☐ Schedule any health maintenance appointments.
☐ Schedule any long-term program you need to correct whatever serious illness may be afflicting you.

Friends
❏ Are the people with whom you spend your time the ones you really enjoy?
❏ When will you make your next efforts to be near those you prefer?

Family
❏ What place will your close relatives have in your new life?
❏ Schedule a time for letting them know their importance.

Reputation
❏ How are you now known? By what words and phrases do people describe you?
❏ Is this how you want to be known?
❏ When will you stand for who you really are?

Spirituality or Tradition
❏ Does your new life honor your spirit?
❏ How does your new life treat the traditions through which you have grown?
❏ How can you honor past and future, society and self?
❏ When will you bring your own true spirit to life? Schedule a day of devotion in your own special style.

Your calendar should be filling up. The appointments you are scheduling, however, are all appointments to live your good new life, the life you envisioned with your Seed Images. Each item you have scheduled should bring release of past burdens, money for the future, time to enjoy your pleasures, and fresh beginnings of health, good relationship, satisfying work, and a home which nourishes you.

Scheduling, not just making a "to do" list, but scheduling "when," is the secret of accomplishing anything. "To do" lists should be made only with a specific date at the top, like "Today, August 11th" or "January 1995." Should an emergency arise which keeps you from accomplishing any scheduled activity, reschedule it. Do not merely say, "I blew it." You never blow it; you only reschedule for a later time. If you find a certain item is habitually rescheduled, ask yourself if you would prefer to get rid of it altogether, and decide exactly when you will.

It may seem like there is so much to schedule this year. Remind yourself, this is the year of your big transition from the life of dissatisfaction to the life of fulfillment. Once you pass through this new course you are charting for yourself you will find it tends to self-fulfill for years afterward.

Accomplishment Eight - Heal Thyself

Many people are used to managing their lives by disaster. They simply attend to the most immediate crisis until it is resolved then go on to the next one. Allowing crisis to chart your course makes for a life of interesting surprises, but they are seldom ones you will enjoy.

A second way of managing one's life is by letting others make the rules. This seems easy because the others carry the burden of decision-making. It seems to work well either when you like their decisions or when you enjoy the act of rebellion. This is often a strong childhood pattern and keeps you a child until you decide to manage your life yourself.

This is what you are beginning to do now. Although self-management carries the responsibility of decision-making, you can see that each decision will be made in your very best interests. You are the decision-maker. You are the boss.

Whether or not you own your own business is hardly the point of this book. You can be employed by someone else and with a shift of attitude realize that you are or can become the most important person on the staff, even without getting a promotion. You promote yourself in your mind to manager of your area of expertise, and as you recognize your worth and perfect your skills you become irreplaceable. Once you know you are irreplaceable, you are in a position to negotiate salary, hours, and title until you have exactly the situation you desire.

Once you are self-managing, whether or not you are employed by someone else loses its security hold over you. With or without a salaried job, you are capable of taking stock of resources and capabilities and putting every last one of them to good use. Also, all of your letting go of past burdens has prepared you to leave an unsatisfactory job should that need to take place.

Whether or not you work for someone else right now, realize that you are in business for yourself. You are charting your course for the year. You have a driving force, your Seed Ideas, and you know the exact days when pieces of this vision shall be fulfilled. They are scheduled on your calendar.

You can be employed by someone else and with a shift of attitude realize that you are or can become the most important person on the staff, even without getting a promotion.

Important Success Tool #8 is the knowledge that images guide. You must realize that the Vision evolving from your Seed Ideas collage is something to be lived piece by piece, day by day, and is not the equivalent of a goal to be achieved somewhere off in the distant future. It is a force causing you to enrich your life, to heal, to renew, perhaps to set short-term goals that you know you can achieve, but it is not something to wait for nor to struggle to get. The Seed Vision must live in your imagination inspiring you, subtly shifting and changing as you grow, always a little beyond your reach, for this is the nature of a driving force. You must allow this Vision to become ever more beautiful with age, and, indeed, it will carry your life into that beauty. But you will never clap your hands and say, "I am done; now I can begin to enjoy." Enjoyment must come every step of the way.

The very first 50 cents dropped into a porcelain cottage-shaped bank that symbolizes your future home or the sea shell on your mantle that brings back the memory of your walk on the beach looking for "your land" must fulfill you. It is certain they will if each step, as I have suggested, is done with you in mind. You decided which bank, which beach, which day, with whom, how much. If you decided with respect for your own likes and desires, then even the smallest decision, the simplest act, will have brought you pleasure.

Never give up the small pleasure for the distant goal. Instead, give up everything outside the realm of your Seed Vision so the vision can become you. As you let go of the rest, your day will still contain spills and turns and surprises, but you will find you have enjoyed them all.

Healing from the Seed Vision is something that happens every day as you stop giving up that which truly nourishes you and begin to live your appointments with health, freedom, saving, and savoring. It is not an end state. It starts here with you taking charge of all the small things which make up your daily life.

Look once again at your Seed Idea collage. Rearrange, add or eliminate any elements which need changing in light of the knowledge you have gained thus far. Healing means to make whole. You are creating a whole new life, a life which recognizes all areas of your human concern and gives each their due. If something is missing from your Seed Vision, add it now.

Review - Accomplishment Eight

Eight - Have you accounted for 1) major relationship, 2) present job, 3) present home, 4) personal health, 5) friends, 6) family, 7) reputation, and 8) spirituality or tradition? Heal the whole.

Healing - Make each small decision in your best interests with your Seed Vision in mind.

Important Success Tool #8 - Know images guide you. Use them to heal.

Relationship Plan:

I graduate from my present job on:

My home, to suit me, needs:

My health plan is:

The friends I will enjoy this year include:

The part my family plays in my new life is:

I most hear people refer to me as:

My work reflects my spirituality by:

The Guide

As you become more certain of the work you want to be doing to maintain the life you intend to live, you will notice that others have walked the path before you. They may have done it with a slightly different style, in a different time or place, but each one has learned lessons on the path and, more than likely, would enjoy sharing their wisdom.

Even though your way will have significant differences than the way of your guide, be open to learning what you can from any person who has succeeded in any portion of the career or lifestyle you are exploring. Even those who have tried and failed may have invaluable knowledge that could keep you from making the same mistakes.

There are books on just about every subject you can think of. Begin reading everything that relates to your area of interest. Your goal must be to become the best of a particular kind of whatever it is you are choosing to become. By this I mean, for example, if you are a musician, your goal must be something like, "I will be the best trumpet player available for Christmas services in southwestern Indianapolis," rather than, "I will be the best musician." The best musician may be your inspiration. The best trumpet player may be your mentor. But you need to locate your own terrain. You decide on the location in which you will practice your art until you have the highest reputation for a particular thing in that location. Only then need you consider enlarging your area, setting your sights on a higher goal.

Accomplishment Nine - Be Guided

In addition to reading in your area of interest, bring yourself into contact with others practicing in your field. Observe and learn from them. Befriend those you are drawn toward. Do not pretend to be as good as those who are more experienced than you. Know the benefits of following. If you think you are better than those who travelled the path before you, your mind will miss the knowledge they have to give. Certain aspects of your talent may exceed those of your guides, but assuming your guide does inspire you, look for her area of expertise and pay attention. If you already knew it all, you would not be reading this book. Let humility guide you into the subtleties of learning that you would otherwise miss.

Often, those who are masters of their craft would like nothing more than to encourage and assist a talented follower. "To follow" means "to come after," to travel the path behind the one who walks ahead. Do not let the term intimidate you. The best learning situations are often those between a wise elder and an enthusiastic yet humble student.

Your chance to guide, to be the leader in your field, will come when others seek the wisdom of your experience. These may be customers, clients, students or apprentices. But you will not know how to treat them unless you have been in their position. If in their position you never encountered a wise elder, your own teaching and guidance will suffer. You will only know how "not" to be. If, on the other hand, you have formed a good relationship with your own mentor, you will have been positively in touch, on a very physical level, with how to properly guide others.

Often, those who are masters of their craft would like nothing more than to encourage and assist a talented follower.

Read the trade journals of your field. Research texts by or about the great ones of your profession. Is there a model you can follow? Is there a human being you can contact? The path is easier to tread in the footprints of those who light the way.

Review - Accomplishment Nine

Nine - Find nine others who preceded you on your path.
Guide - Choose one to listen to attentively.
Important Success Tool #9 - Know when to be humble.

My Mentors

List nine possible guides, mentors, or exemplary examples in your field in column 1. In column 2, list how or where you might find each one. In column 3, enter when you will do this. In column 4, enter their response to your interest.

Mentors	How/where	When	Response
1.			
2.			
3.			
4.			
5.			
6.			
7.			
8.			
9.			

Harvest

Pay attention to your typical day. Each experience is the result of decisions you made awhile back. The average day you experience is the harvest of thousands of thoughts, desires, longings, repressions, and expressions. Is the harvest good? Do you have plenty of the kinds of moments you enjoy? Take stock of your routine.

Look at getting up in the morning, for example. Is it to the sound of birds at just the time your body feels like awakening? Is it to the excitement of a full day of activities in which you have wanted to participate for a long time? Is it to the smell of fresh bread or to the feeling of satin sheets? How would you like it to be? On your way to the bathroom, do you have time to notice the sun streaming through your favorite lace curtains? Do you pass by the book-in-process you were writing before you went to bed? Do you hear the voices of children? What is everything saying to you? Will you sit down to your favorite breakfast or jump into the car you always wanted and drive to meet a friend to share the special blend of coffee she recommended?

It is the small events of life that make up the day. How consciously have you chosen the tiny seeds of habit that form the core of your life? Have you allowed yourself to have a favorite chair? A proper desk? A vehicle that always gets you where you want to go? An acceptable shirt? A pleasant route to the store? Conversation which nourishes you at dinner? The tools of your trade? How many little things have you given up for one reason or another?

Most of your life is spent in habitual routines. If all of these are without frills, do you expect a night at the movies or a dinner out to make up for this lack?

Most of your life is spent in habitual routines like sleeping, personal hygiene, going to and fro, cooking, eating, and maintenance of your material surroundings. If all of these are without frills, do you expect a night at the movies or a dinner out to make up for this lack? What might life be like if you gave these everyday activities special embellishments? Perhaps you would need little other entertainment. Perhaps you would not feel the longing for a different job, a different place, a different partner.

Accomplishment Ten - Arrange a Bountiful Harvest

Once again, gaze at your Seed Vision. Of what would your daily routine consist in that ideal life? How would the environment for each routine activity look if it were just right? What small things pleasure you? How much order feels good? What measure of spontaneity would be present in this orderly life?

Begin changing the smallest things to suit your liking. Change your toothpaste or your bedspread or the roads you drive to work. Give yourself a fresh new something in place of what you no longer enjoy. Keep replacing the worn-out experience with whatever perks up your mind. Set your harvest table with what is best for you.

With each exercise you are shifting all of the subtle energies of life to realign in support of your Seed Vision, the new fulfilling life you want to live. Never underestimate the power of these small changes. As you make them in your own life, you will become more aware of how these small daily occurrences affect your clients or customers as well. In your store or office you will begin to pay attention to what makes your visitor feel welcome. Each time a potential customer enters your domain, you present them with the bounty of that which you have prepared for them. Make it be what you would enjoy.

The basic nature of our Earth is that of providing plenty. This must be your attitude toward your clients, your customers, and yourself as well. Success is an appreciation of the wealth which surrounds us. If you are living your personal life in a way which allows the small pleasures of the day, you will be inclined to provide the little extras that give your clients the feeling that what you offer is the very best for them.

Your private life and your public business reflect each other. This is true whether you act on stage before an audience of thousands or only appear before the public as a product in a catalog. Business is putting yourself out in the public eye. It is possible to pretend, to have a false front, but this is not the life you are trying to achieve. You want to feel congruent, to be wholly present in what you do. You are seeking integration of Earth and Spirit, the material and the transpersonal aspects of your life. The only way to get such holistic fulfillment is to start small at home with the tiniest seeds of that which you deem beautiful.

Review - Accomplishment Ten

Ten - Surround yourself with small and beautiful experiences.

Harvest - You are reaping what you have sown. Give your clients or customers the feeling that they have just entered the domain of plenty and are about to reap a bountiful harvest. Do the same for yourself. **Important Success Tool #10** - The extra little touch.

The extra touch I can add now is:

Balance

As you see the implications of your life's effect on others and the environment, make any changes necessary to allow a balance of benefit. You are a part of the world; there is no escape. You are having an impact. You can analyze that impact. In what ways does your new lifestyle and business help the planet? How does it benefit your community? Are there changes that would create more good for others without hurting your personal well-being?

Life requires that we constantly choose both life and death. We eat to stay alive, but to do so we take the life of plants or animals. We build homes to stay warm, but our homes take trees. We wear natural fibers, but these are sometimes grown in ways which deplete the soil.

It is impossible to have a totally clean slate. But we are bound to live according to our conscience, to attempt to carry out our ideals.

Accomplishment Eleven - Balance Your Energy Investments

Review your ecological ideals. Are they doable? How about your relationship ideals? Are you taking into account the state of your society? Are you being realistic in light of the current state of world and cultural affairs? You are doing your life within a context of time, location, and societal mores. There is no way to truly keep your decisions from having an influence, nor to isolate yourself from the influence of the world upon your decisions.

You are a part of the world; there is no escape. You are having an impact.

Many a young woman has left her hard won homestead behind after years of labor when she finally realized that she could not live in social isolation. Likewise, many a business has folded because it was a good idea whose time had not yet come. In other words, the entrepreneur did not pay attention to what the market was ready to accept.

Think about what you have to offer the world right now. What is your business? What good is it? Whether you are already employed or are starting your own business, these are important questions to ask yourself. What are you willing to give the world, and is the world ready for it? What talents and skills do you have to offer, and who needs them right now?

In your ultimate ideal life, you may fantasize never working. Destroy this myth now. A life without work is humanly impossible. You may enjoy your work so that it seems like play. Or, you may work hard a few hours and have fun many. But you cannot live without working. Everyone requires food, clothing, and shelter, however simple it may be. Everyone exerts energy to acquire these.

Gathering food, clothing, and shelter is a basic drive. Creating food, clothing, and shelter is craftsmanship. Embellishing them is art. Exchanging and accounting for them is business. We are all more or less involved in each of these activities. Even an heir to private fortunes must make some exchanges and accounting for what she receives. Make peace with this fact of life. Work is.

A second myth to destroy is, "Because I am a good person, everything I need will come to me." Perhaps, if you were lucky, that was true in your childhood. Mom and Dad reward good behavior in a material way. Unless they are still treating you this way, thus keeping you a child, this axiom is no longer true. You are an adult now. And though you may still choose to be good in the moral and behavioral sense of the phrase, being good no longer equals material gain.

This is often a tough lesson to learn. But your initiation as a person of power requires it. We have all been told so often to "be good" that there is a danger that we will believe the world is set up to magically provide for us if we are just nice people. Think about it. How many totally wonderful, talented, dedicated, honest, brave, brilliant human beings have suffered "unfair" treatment. The number is staggering.

Your immediate family may have been structured to reward good behavior. That was then. Understand this now. You are no longer a child. Though a child of God or child of the Spirit still in many ways, in the world, you are grown up. And it is in the world and from the world that you must make your living. To paraphrase an old saying, "You must give to the Spirit what is the Spirit's and to the world what is the world's." Give G.O.D. your love, devotion, and dedication of all you do. Be wise and kind in your dealings. Do all you believe in. Live your deeply felt values. But work in the world by its rules.

In other words, mere intention accomplishes little. Beautiful fantasies and desires get nothing done. Being a perfect mother and pristine housekeeper never paid a bill. Sacrificing your talent's expression so that someone else can get ahead leaves you still behind. Of course, thoughtless action is wrong. Work without a dream is demeaning. You are after balance. Be good for God/Goddess/All

That Is, and be savvy about work.

"Being good" when you were five years old meant keeping clean and acting nice. "Being good" at 35 means increasing your skill at what you do until you are an expert. You might be both. But do not fall into the trap of thinking that sweetness equals success.

Without these myths to sap your energy, you can more easily look at the various aspects of life that require your attention. To do this we will use the model of the Medicine Wheel containing the teachings of the Four Directions. Each direction, north, east, south, and west, has a particular energy associated with it. These energies correspond to nature. As you observe nature then, you can easily and ongoingly bring your life into balance. Nature keeps a certain cycle of renewal happening. You are wise if you keep this cycle of renewal happening in yourself. Let us look at where you are investing your energy now, in terms of the Medicine Wheel.

Beginning with the eastern quadrant, Spring asks you to allow time to fantasize and become inspired by great possibilities. Then, put your talent behind your Vision and develop your craft into its highest art form. You will always be a desirable employee or a successful self-employed person if you continually improve your skills. Be the best you can be. Everything needs the inspiration of a fresh look from time to time. From the East comes enthusiasm, the energy to begin. You overuse the East energy when you continually start things and never get beyond start-up.

Next, in the southern quadrant, you begin to plan, to formulate your ideas and fit them into your overall philosophy of life. you see how the new idea can enhance the overall picture. You create a form through which the idea can be carried out. You begin working out the bugs and taking everything as far as you can. You attend to details. You get rid of those parts of the original idea that are not workable. The South is the energy of will-to-do, what you are used to thinking of as will power. You have decided your Spring idea was worth doing and you have begun the process of carrying it through. You misuse South energy when you do not know when to quit.

The West is all about quitting. It is time out. Time to reflect, look

back, reconsider, take a rest. It is the Fall. Think of it, if you will, as falling into a comfortable chair and looking over what you have done so far. Get the big picture, checking out the spiritual or invisible aspects of your project. Is it worth completing? Are you loving it? Is it beneficial to others? Will you continue to enjoy the process and the product?

Whatever it is that you spend your time working on becomes, in a sense, the object of your devotion. You devote your time and energy. Devotion is a spiritual act. Devote your time and energy to something you want to offer the Great Spirit. Your whole working life then becomes a devotion to the One You Love. You will find your work fulfilling to the extent that you dedicate all of those hours of labor to whatever entity you deeply admire and desire. Even if you have no particular belief in God, a devotion and dedication of your work to some greater cause than yourself will make everything feel so much more worthwhile. The West is asking you to make this spiritual commitment and giving you time to think about it. This is the quadrant of spiritual love, that love which gives without regard to receiving.

Now remember, this is just one fourth of the wheel. This giving without receiving is only a part of life. The East says, "Here have a bunch of Spring energy, free, uplifting, abundant." The South says, "Great, now do something with it." The West says, "Good job, now who was that for?" And the North comes along to accept any errors and prepare for a clean start.

Although you can put your generous spirit into everything you do, you cannot operate a business without also participating in fair exchange. This is the concern of the North. Here you enter into contracts. "I will give you this if you give me that." You and your customers, or anyone with whom you have a contractual relationship must both feel fairly treated. This applies to your relationship contract with the planet as well.

You gather resources from Earth. With them you must create something which will encourage her ability to provide those resources ongoingly. You must be a part of a cycle of eternal fertility, for this is what she desires. The least of your obligations is to recycle waste.

90

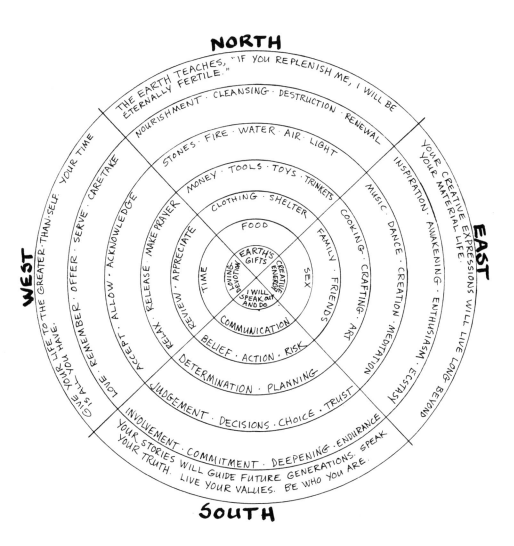

NORTH

THE EARTH TEACHES, "IF YOU REPLENISH ME, I WILL BE ETERNALLY FERTILE."

NOURISHMENT · CLEANSING · DESTRUCTION · RENEWAL

STONES · FIRE · WATER · AIR · LIGHT

MONEY · TOOLS · TOYS · TRINKETS

CLOTHING · SHELTER

FOOD

EARTH'S GIFTS / CREATIVE ENERGY

LOVING DEVOTION

I WILL SPEAK OUT AND DO

TIME

SEX

FAMILY · FRIENDS

COOKING · CRAFTING · ART

MUSIC · DANCE · CREATION · MEDITATION

INSPIRATION · AWAKENING · ENTHUSIASM · ECSTASY

YOUR CREATIVE EXPRESSIONS WILL LIVE LONG BEYOND YOUR MATERIAL LIFE.

EAST

COMMUNICATION

BELIEF · ACTION · RISK

DETERMINATION · PLANNING

JUDGEMENT · DECISIONS · CHOICE · TRUST

INVOLVEMENT · COMMITMENT · DEEPENING · ENDURANCE. SPEAK YOUR STORIES WILL GUIDE FUTURE GENERATIONS. YOUR TRUTH. LIVE YOUR VALUES. BE WHO YOU ARE.

REVIEW · APPRECIATE

RELAX · MAKE PRAYER

ACCEPT · RELEASE · ALLOW · ACKNOWLEDGE

CARETAKE

REMEMBER · OFFER · SERVE ·

LOVE · GIVE YOUR LIFE TO THE GREATER-THAN-SELF. YOUR TIME IS ALL YOU HAVE.

WEST

SOUTH

91

Beyond that, all decisions regarding use of material resources must consider their effect on seven generations. This is the way of all people who have sustained their cultures for thousands of years. You have a contract with the planet; she is not merely your spiritual mother.

Everything you have has the Earth Mother as its source. She provides every resource you use. Along the way, artists and craftspeople have shaped each object, and merchants have exchanged the item for another thing of value. Each hand gives and receives. These transactions are basic to life and culture. They need to be respected and appreciated. Caring for every material possession and expressing caring in every transaction are essential to being blessed in business.

> *Whatever it is that you spend your time working on becomes, in a sense, the object of your devotion.*

True prosperity comes from love, the caring interactions and cared for things that circulate through our lives bringing us what we need at all times. Real wealth is an abundant planet and creative people acting in respect for the great circle of life. Do your part, or die. This is the ultimate lesson of the North, place of death and preparation for rebirth. It is Winter on the Medicine Wheel. It is the dark of night. It is the emptiness. If you cannot go on, it absorbs you into itself.

Study the wheel. Are you giving each direction its due? Are you keeping the circle whole? Life is a gift. You receive energy, resources and kin with which to make art of life. You are given will to pass through challenges. And here and there, you are asked to pause and offer what you have made of life to the One Beyond Yourself. Over and over around the wheel, you go through many small deaths, the emptying which prepares you for starting over, until the final death we all must share.

Review - Accomplishment Eleven

Eleven - One to one, we are all here in relation to each other.
Balance - The energy of each direction must be acknowledged.
Important Success Tool #11 - The Medicine Wheel, the four powers of nature.

Here is how my business helps the planet:

Here is how my business helps the community:

Vision

Your Seed Vision is carrying you along now, having evolved from your original inspiration. The exercises in this book have asked you to take some good long looks at your life and the business you do each day. You may see that there are realities to face, responsibilities that you find yourself obliged to keep up for a long time to come. There may be very real limitations to your physical capabilities. You may wonder if you can get past the obstacles. Or, you may have found your Seed Vision to be merely a glimpse of what you now see as amazing possibilities. Perhaps both are true.

You can use the Four Powers Medicine Wheel on the following page as a graphic way to assess your physical, emotional, mental, and

NORTH - YOUR PHYSICAL SITUATION

EAST - YOUR CREATIVE VITALITY

WEST - YOUR RELATIONSHIP TO SPIRIT

SOUTH - YOUR MENTAL PROWESS

VIOLET: I RECYCLE, RE-USE, RESTORE AND REPAIR. I AM A CARETAKER OF PLANETARY RESOURCES.

INDIGO: MY WORK IS OF BENEFIT TO LIFE. I HONOR OTHER LIFE FORMS AND MY HUMAN SISTERS AND BROTHERS.

BLUE: I EXPRESS MY VALUES IN MY HOME, MY WORK, AND MY LIFESTYLE. EARTH IS NOURISHED BY THE WAY I LIVE.

GREEN: I HAVE COMMITTED TO A GEOGRAPHIC LOCATION AND I AM PUTTING MY HEART INTO IT.

YELLOW: I LET OTHERS KNOW WHAT I HAVE TO OFFER.

ORANGE: I TAKE CARE OF MY BODY AND BASIC NEEDS.

RED: I AM I. I ACCEPT MYSELF.

I TRUST LIFE.

I CAN SAY "YES"

I CAN SAY "NO"

I REALIZE MY LIMITATIONS.

I CAN DEFEND MYSELF.

I SUPPORT THOSE I BELIEVE IN.

I PRACTICE AND PERFECT MY SKILLS AND TALENTS.

I PLAN, ORGANIZE AND ORDER MY LIFE.

I PRIORITIZE AND ECONOMIZE RESOURCES.

I SEEK BROADER KNOWLEDGE. I STUDY AND RESEARCH MY FIELD. I ACCEPT THOSE AHEAD OF ME AND THOSE BEHIND.

I HAVE FULLY COMMITTED TO A PATH AND PROCEED TO THE BEST OF MY ABILITY.

I FEEL AT PEACE IN NATURE.

I ACCEPT MY PAST, THE SPIRIT OF MY CHILDHOOD.

I GO TOWARD OTHERS.

I EXTERNALIZE MY LOVE BY WHAT WORKS AND KINDNESS.

I AM A BENEFICIAL FORCE WHICH RESPECTS ALL BEINGS.

I FOLLOW MY INTUITION. I BELIEVE I AM GUIDED.

I TRUST THE VOICE WITHIN ME.

MY DEVOTION TAKES TANGIBLE FORM (RITUAL)

IN SERVING ANOTHER AS IN SERVING MYSELF, I FEEL AS MUCH PLEASURE.

I SEE GOD EVERYWHERE. OFTEN, I HAVE THE COURAGE TO LET OTHERS SEE WHO I REALLY AM.

I EXPRESS QUALITY AND BEAUTY IN MY WORK.

I MAKE FRIENDS. I CARE ABOUT THEM.

I EXPRESS AFFECTION TO THOSE I LOVE. I GET INVOLVED.

I AM ENTHUSIASTIC. I ENJOY SINGING, DANCING AND PLAYING MUSIC.

I IMAGINE GREAT POSSIBILITIES. I ENVISION A GLORIOUS FUTURE.

I CREATIVELY PURSUE MY ARTISTIC INTERESTS. I MAKE ART OF LIFE.

I DREAM AND

96

spiritual strengths. With a colored pencil or crayon, shade in each segment of the wheel according to the strength you feel in that area, very lightly if it is weak, heavily if it is strong. Do the same for each quadrant, the North reflecting your physical situation, the East depicting your creative energy and vitality for living, the South depicting your mental prowess and the West showing your depth of relationship to the spirit.

When you are finished, you will see certain light areas. You need to decide whether or not these areas are A) ones which you can change with a reasonable effort that you are willing to expend, or B) ones which cannot be changed other than by acts of God or just are not worth the energy they would require. For the A's, make a list of the possible ways to create the desired change. For the B's consider who you know who excels in that area and what you might exchange with them in order to receive their services. See the "Who To Hire" chart for examples.

Accomplishment Twelve - Get the Big Vision

What you are doing here is facing reality and finding out where you need help. Where will you <u>always</u> need an assistant to strengthen the balanced life you wish to lead. Being human is the equivalent of having limitations. But with awareness of what these are and the ability to form contractual relationships, all of our human needs are filled.

It is a waste of time, your very precious gift from life itself, to indulge in self-criticism other than as a momentary awareness to facilitate a correction. Ongoing low self-esteem is like a hole in your gas tank. Plug it up right now. In the areas of your limitations, someone else excels. Hire them. And do not hire other unskilled help except as a charitable contribution where you expect nothing in return. Hire people that you feel are better than you in the areas in which you are weak. This frees you to put your total energy into your true talents.

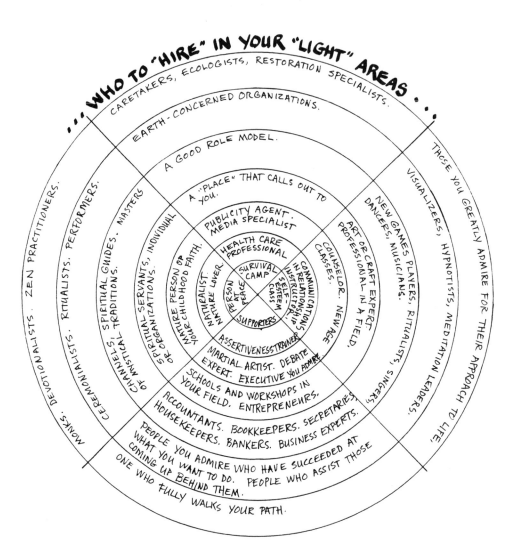

Remember that hiring does not necessarily mean taking on an employee. It may mean contracting with an existing business firm which specializes in the area of your need. It could mean trading skills with a competent friend. Or it may mean simply letting your partner do what he or she is good at and staying out of the way. America is a do-it-yourself society. It is sometimes difficult for us to give up our involvement in something even if we are no good at it. Your business success depends upon overcoming this tendency. You need the best person for each job which needs to be done. It may not be you.

On the other hand, be sure to note the strong areas you have colored in on the Four Powers Medicine Wheel. This is who you are. These are your powers. Put them to work where they will do you and the world the most good.

> *In the areas of your limitations, someone else excels. Hire them.*

Now that you have a clear picture of yourself, go for an outing alone in nature. Face the wild world one on one. Be alone with the Mother Earth. Have a talk with life. Make a prayer from the depths of your being saying in your own words, "This is who I am. This is how you created me. These are my talents which I wish to give to the world. From Creator they have come as gifts, and I have added to them by my life study and experience. I am embarking on a new course which will use them fully and will draw upon my every resource. I am ready to become a woman (or man) of power. Please guide me. Offer me your direction. To this I am now open." Then be silent for a long time.

Review - Accomplishment Twelve

Twelve - The end of childhood, the beginning of wisdom.
Vision - Prepare to become your full adult self.
Important Success Tool #12 - Know your limitations. In those areas, hire only those who are better than you.

Sunset

When you pass through a series of systematic changes such as you are going through now, it is easy to lose sight of where you began. In your notebook, it is helpful to keep some reminders. You might enjoy keeping a daily journal of the emerging you. Or you may just want to record financial changes and business trends as you adjust your management style.

I suggest that you at least dig out a copy of last year's income tax statement so that you know where you were financially, and take one more sheet of paper to make a note about how you felt earning that year's income. When you again make this assessment at the end of the coming year, you will see a remarkable difference.

I cannot know whether you will have doubled your income, but if you have wholeheartedly done the exercises in this book, you will be feeling the prosperity of being in charge of a happy life. You will have become your own boss whether or not you are employed by someone else. The old life of feeling overpowered by circumstances beyond your control will have passed into the sunset.

Lesson Thirteen - Let the Sunset Dissolve Your Sorrows

Every sunset is a good time to ask yourself what you need to release for the day. There are several ways to look at this question. What can I do to release any pent-up emotions I have neglected to express today? Perhaps a run around the block, a swim, or a shout (but not <u>at</u> anyone) will do the job.

> *A ritual can be created around any activity simply by generating a focused intent.*

Ask yourself, "What do I see in my daily routine that appears to be no longer useful? Where did I get caught in old binds, and how can I relieve the squeeze?" As you begin your releasing activity, whether it is a hot bath or a mental accounting, do it in a ritual manner.

A ritual can be created around any activity simply by generating a focused intent, for example, "I am now going to do (this) to release (that)." Bring all of your awareness to that intent and keep it there. This can be done by having a running dialogue with yourself. Just keep making up sentences which express how and what you are releasing, such as, "I am beginning now to look at this tension in my head. Now I am realizing it came about lunchtime when Mr. Smith came in. I am now shouting what I wished I could have said to him. There, that felt good. Now, I allow the image of Mr. Smith to dissolve, just as the sound of my voice has dissolved into the air. I see myself now removing any imaginary ribbons of energy tied to Mr. Smith's problem. I feel the relaxation beginning. I take off my shoes. I loosen my shirt.

I sit near the sunny window. I observe nature. I am glad to be living here. I love the tree I planted over there last year. I am so glad it is spring."

Just keep talking to yourself, describing everything as you steer your attention toward release of the negative and observation of the positive. This is attention management. It is very important in ritual action. Every warrior must have this ability. Every medicine person must constantly call upon this ability. Your business requires that you continually observe problems and steer the situation toward solutions. Now, use your concentration to heal yourself.

At a certain point, you will just get lost in some positive feeling you have guided yourself toward, such as, focusing on the budding tree as spring approaches. The next thing you will be aware of is that you had not been thinking of anything for quite a few minutes. Your consciousness has been lifted from the mundane and brought up to the level of the eternal. You are floating in some experience of quality. You have become one with the spirit of something. The sunset itself, if you can see it each day, provides just such a possibility for upliftment.

After your awareness returns to the everyday, make some small action which acknowledges the gift you have just received. Touch the Earth. Make a prayer. Do a sketch. Write a poem. Whatever feels like an outpouring of your feeling of appreciation. Play around with different possibilities until you find the one most rewarding.

Rituals are ways of making statements to your body, mind, and spirit that you are passing from one phase to another. They are transition markers just like the dawn of a new day and the setting of the sun on the day past. They mark points of fresh starts and new opportunities as well as releases and endings. Without meaningful ending ritual, one just goes on running like an errant vacuum cleaner whose bag is never emptied. Without ritual of new starts, there is no feeling of growth, no marking of time and the approach of wisdom.

As you make cleansing and releasing ritual a part of your life, you will notice a difference in your energy. Other people will also enjoy being around you more. Remember, a daily shower can be just as powerful as a fancy religious ceremony if you clear your mind and fully release your emotions with your clearing intent in mind.

Find what works for you. Make it a special time with special objects or in a special place. It need only take a few minutes. Symbolize what is passing. Symbolize what is coming. This can be in material form or just in your mind. In this way, you become complete emotionally. You gain a feeling of closure and your energy is free to take up the new day and the new opportunity.

Review - Accomplishment Thirteen

Thirteen - Change is inevitable. Honor it.
Sunset - Release the day in a ritual way.
Important Success Tool #13 - Personal ritual.

My ritual consists of the following:

1) the object symbolic of my frustration:

2) the 1-5 minute action I am taking to release it:

3) the object symbolic of my new freedom from this frustration:

4) the 5-10 minute peaceful act of enjoyment:

Blend

Being in business is being constantly vigilant of the marketplace. The marketplace is people, their perceived needs, what they currently enjoy, why they think they enjoy it, how they like to enjoy it. The marketplace has nothing to do with what YOU think people OUGHT to think, do or want. It is not your job to preach a right way, but to observe and to take those observations into your creative mind.

There can certainly be ideals you wish people would follow, ways they could act to make this a better world. You need your values. They guide you in your decisions. And it is alright to wish everyone were right there with you, doing it the same way. But you will only help people to adopt your way of thinking by noticing where they are and creating a path they can follow to change.

If you are already in the role of a minister or a political activist, you do have more license to preach than the average person. It is part of your job and people expect it from you. They accept and value you in this role. Even at this extreme, however, you will make greater headway if you pay attention to the marketplace.

> *Marketing is the act of looking at the people you most want to serve and providing a service they will perceive as valuable.*

Look at people. Look at the people you want to serve. Who are they? What are they looking for? How can you open a door for them? How can you provide a part of their path? What product or service can you offer which will lead them toward your mutually beneficial ideal? Marketing is the act of looking at the people you most want to serve and providing a service they will perceive as valuable.

Marketing is blending, mixing a little of your talents and desires with a portion of the world's needs. It is not charging ahead with an idea only you love. It is not giving up what you love in order to please someone else. It is the perfect blend of your need to express your true self and society's need to have access to your creative energy.

Accomplishment Fourteen - Blend With Your People

Look again at who you are. Observe the photo of you in your Seed Vision collage. Recollect your skills and talents. Then think about who you enjoy relating to: the poor and downtrodden? the mildly troubled? the average American? the ladies of the church? the New Age shamans? the truck drivers of America? the Little League baseball teams? the artists who work with fiber?

As you can see, the list of possibilities is endless. You need to

106

locate a particular market segment that you can enjoy dealing with. Never enter a career just because the money is good or the client group is needy. Your customers and clients are going to be in your life every day in one way or another. You might as well make them people you enjoy.

After you define your market, ask yourself, what is the best way to reach them with what I have to offer? Where are they? How can I get my product there? What are they inclined to notice and respond to? What will they want from me? What can I give them that no one else is giving them in the way I can give it? What do I need in return? Carefully consider each of these questions and blend the real you with a segment of the real world.

Review - Accomplishment Fourteen

Fourteen - Know yourself (and your product or service).
Blend - Look to see who is asking for you (and your product or service).
Important Success Tool #14 - A market (your client group). Test: do you have fourteen people who want what you offer?

Marketplace Blend

In column 1, enter the kinds of people you enjoy relating to. In column 2, enter the item or service <u>they</u> think they need (your own best guess will do for now). In column 3, enter what you have to offer them that relates to their need. In column 4, enter the dollar amount you need which they might agree to give you in exchange for your product or service. Trading for other goods or services is also possible.

Client/customer Group	They think they need:	I have to offer:	They will give for my service:

The Trickster

As you move out into the world with your new, freshly balanced self, you may feel that the world should notice. Now that you have brought your life together and decided to give of your wondrous being to those who really need you, you may expect them to be appreciative. You may think that the time and energy you have devoted to taking control of your financial situation should entitle you to the privilege of a business start-up loan or a raise or some praise. However, the world may not immediately respond.

The Trickster is at work. A test is taking place. This is a test to check out just how satisfying your life has become even without external reward.

Accomplishment Fifteen - Be Wise to the Trickster

If you have arranged your days to your liking, rid yourself of obstacles to the expression of your true being, have begun to manage and appreciate your current resources, and have created a pleasant space for yourself, your life should be feeling good even if external recognition is missing. There should be a growing feeling inside you that says, "I don't care if I don't get a financial payoff, I would not want to live any other way."

Once that state of being is accomplished, doors will begin to open for you. Some of the openings will lead you to unexpected new wonders. It will be a time of pleasant surprises. These may be well-deserved, but, having become used to less-than-optimum conditions, you may tend to reject them. At this point, you may have to do a little psychological work on letting yourself fully receive. I call this, increasing your tolerance for bliss.

> *At this point, you may have to do a little psychological work on letting yourself fully receive. I call this, increasing your tolerance for bliss.*

Assuming you can pass this Trickster's first test, a second test will come. The stage is set something like the following: You have spent many years excluded from the realm of business or expertise into which you are now entering. Your exclusion gave you an outsider's view of the business world. An outsider's view is always a simplified abstract or idealized view. It does not know how the business realm works day to day behind the scenes.

An example with which you might be familiar is that of a student leaving college and "book" learning to embark on a real world career. She will have much to learn about the specific how-to's of her new job, and some of these how-to's will not go "by the book."

The Trickster is now going to introduce you to how it is REALLY done. You may meet characters you did not imagine actually existed. You may encounter crooks, loan sharks, incompetents, rip-off artists, totally uncaring people, people who value little what you value highly. You may be shocked or frightened. You pass the test when you recognize you only have to manage yourself.

This is an ethical check point in your journey. Many complex situations will be offered where right and wrong are not black and white. The Trickster is asking you to think deeply about your own values. This is a reality check of your untested ideals.

You might find that you need to temper some of your opinions. There will be some areas where you see that you expected the impossible or just did not know the way things were usually done. You might see that your client group encompasses more kinds of people than you thought it would. You might be faced with a law that interferes with a worthy profession, such as midwifery, or asks you to be licensed at a cost too high to pay.

There will be times when you will say, "I will do it your way, even though I thought I could do it mine." There will be times when you will say, "This is too important for me to change. It is basic to my values, to my feeling good about myself." What is happening is a firming up of your ethical "bottom line." You are discovering how far you will bend for what reasons, and learning what are your deeply held convictions which you will never compromise.

All ideals, religious convictions, and righteous opinions must be tested in the world. This starts the process of shaping those lofty opinions into functioning goodness. Ideals untested are completely useless to society. The Trickster's tests are for the benefit of humanity as well as your personal enlightenment. Your ideals will be tempered by the fire. This is how it is. But after you get past the coals, you will know who you are.

Review - Accomplishment Fifteen

Fifteen - Have the courage to test your convictions.
Trickster - This is a reality check.
Important Success Tool #15 - Knowing your values work.

My expectations are:

Pierced Shield

You have heard the saying, "Into each life a little rain must fall." This includes your business life. Not everything will work out as you hope it will even with the best planning, keen awareness of market trends, and the most balanced approach. Being in business requires warrior's mind in the sense that you are training yourself in the skills needed to go out into the consumer wilds and overtake a territory called a market niche.

No one <u>really</u> needs any of the millions of products or services on the market. Ancient or so-called primitive people got along just fine without any of the glut of things available to us today. And they managed to keep the Earth a bountiful paradise which gave them more entertainment than the best VCR, Mercedes, or microwave oven can ever do. At any moment, present day consumers may realize they do not need your product. You should always be ready for this time.

Accomplishment Sixteen - Get Ready for the Pierced Shield

Think of the business you are creating as a shield. It protects you from financial need, it provides those things which protect your family. Let us call this business you are creating, Plan A. You are making Plan A as foolproof as you possibly can. But, you must be ready for market shifts, those times when your customers suddenly decide something else is more appropriate for them than your product or service. For these times when your protective business shield is pierced, you need an alternative plan. Let us call this Plan B.

Establish for yourself a security bottom line. That is, ask yourself what is the most basic level you could tolerate living? This security bottom line is Plan B. Make sure it is <u>always</u> in place. For instance, you may feel that in a real pinch, you could get along just fine with a tent, a sleeping bag, a cooking pot, and a bag of rice. You have always loved the freedom of outdoor living and would consider it a pleasant interlude. If this is who you are, get that camping gear now and stash it in your security closet.

On the other hand, you may feel that if things got really bad, you could go home to Mom. See if Mom agrees. Then put some energy into Mom. Help her to be able to help you in the future. Perhaps, there is a family estate or paid-off vacation cabin. If this is an option, make it your responsibility to maintain it as your possible future temporary home.

If you feel incapable of functioning without all of your present modern conveniences, your best bet is to save frugally so that you own everything you really depend upon outright. Pay off all debts on whatever consists of your bottom line security. Then you might enroll in a wilderness survival course just to assure your emotional body that it <u>could</u> keep your physical body alive if it had to.

To know you will always have food and warmth is the bottom line primal level of security. It gives you your basic self-confidence as a human on Earth. With this assurance, establishing the higher levels of self-confidence will be easier.

Life insurance, health insurance, house insurance, retirement plans, savings accounts and the like are all fine if they make sense to you, but they all depend upon the continuation of the present money economy. Nothing could be further from the security I am talking about here. The true foundation of your life is how you gather food and water, keep yourself warm in nature, and how easy it is for you to form relationship with another living being.

> *The true foundation of your life is how you gather food and water, keep yourself warm in nature, and how easy it is for you to form relationship with another living being.*

When you know and trust yourself here at this basic level of self-sustenance, you can go on to work fully in the money economy and do the financial security planning appropriate to your situation. Plan A brings you the money you need to manifest your Seed Vision. Plan A requires that you take some risks, giving up some well-worn patterns in yourself to become all you can be. Plan B makes those risks less risky. Plan B shields you from undue stress day to day, and from total disaster should the worst happen. It is a shield which cannot easily be destroyed by outside forces. Know what you need to make this second shield and see that it is always in order.

Then, with your security closet filled with backpack and boots or your name on the family farm, you can proceed with your most daring plans. You can afford to take risks because you can afford to lose everything else. Of course, you do not plan to lose everything else. You plan as wisely as you can to keep all of your assets and to improve the situation. To help you do the planning you need to do there are age old business tools called Cash Flow Journals. Every time you look at these magic books they will tell you exactly what needs to be done.

The key phrase here is, "look at these magic books." The wise business person, as soon as she sees sales falling or a scheme going awry, quickly looks to how she can patch the hole. She notices the hole immediately because EVERY DAY she looks at income compared to outgo. And every week she compares prior weeks. And every month she compares prior months. And every season and every year she does the same.

Looking at the financial Daily Journal takes only a few minutes. The journal is like a guardian angel reporting to you each day about how you are relating to the world. Relating is a give and take. Sometimes the world gives more than you expected. Sometimes it gives less. The financial Daily Journal keeps you informed. It tells you exactly what it is you are getting and exactly what you are putting out.

To see for yourself, take one of your fourteen column green ledger sheets and head it, "Daily Journal for the Month of _____." Every item on which you spend money needs to be written in at the end of the day. In the left-hand information column, write to whom the check or cash was given. In the next column write the amount, and in the column extensions write the same amount under headings with titles such as Food, Household, Clothing, Office Supplies, etc. At the end of the month, total all of the columns top to bottom to see what you have given the world (cash outlay) in exchange for what it has given you (all the items you purchased).

I suggest you do a separate page in the same manner as a personal energy audit. List in the left-hand column the people or projects to which you gave energy, next to that how many hours, and in the extension, list those same hours under headings such as: Talking On the Phone, Cleaning, Studying, Personal Care, Sleeping, Fun, etc. Both of these Daily Journals should be very enlightening.

A second section of your Daily Journal will be the income section. In the same manner that you have listed outgo, list your financial and energy income. Break it down into headings that fit your particular situation. This might include: Gifts From Mom, Salary From Job, Refunds, Welfare or Child Support, Trade Exchanges, etc. Your personal energy income page may include: Visits From Friends, Extra Attention From Others, Time Off, Dancing, Hot Baths, Watching TV,

Walks in the Country, or whatever your personal pleasures may be.

For now, I am having you combine both business and personal expenses and income in your Daily Journal. This is just to help you to get the Big Picture of where your money is going and to help you see what you are getting for it. Likewise, the personal energy expenses and income pages will show you where your time is going and what pleasures you are receiving for the time you take. You may discover quite an imbalance. You may be putting out much more than you feel you are getting. The journal entries will show you where the energy and financial leaks are. You must become aware of your present spending and receiving habits in order to make wise new decisions. In a month or two, you will be able to reduce your record keeping to just the business income and expenses necessary for informing, planning, and tax purposes. For now, the objective is awareness. Your shield is only as good as your information.

Review - Accomplishment Sixteen

Sixteen - Establish your bottom line security.
Pierced Shield - If you are ready for the worst, it cannot get that bad.
Important Success Tool #16 - The Daily Income and Expense Journal.

117

DAILY JOURNAL FOR THE MONTH OF _____

PAGE 1

	Initials	Date
Prepared By		
Approved By		

WILSON JONES COMPANY   G7514D ColumnWrite ®

DISBURSEMENTS: COLUMNS 2-14

MADE IN U.S.A.

DATE	TO WHOM CHECK WAS WRITTEN (OR CASH)	CHECK (OR CASH) AMOUNT	HOUSE PAYMENT	PHONE & UTILITIES (HEAT, WATER...)	SAVINGS &/or INSURANCE	GARDEN SUPPLIES & SEEDS	FOOD	
JAN. 3	LaSpendola Gifts	5500						1
	Co-op Grocery	3752					3752	2
Jan. 7	Light Stuff Books	1015						3
Jan. 15	Cityville Hall	1702		1702				4
Jan. 30	Marge Landlady	27500	27500					5
	MONTHLY TOTAL	39469	27500	1702	—	—	3752	6

Review: Is your money going where you thought it was?

When you title your Disbursement Columns #2-14, say to yourself, "I

DAILY JOURNAL FOR THE MONTH OF _____

PAGE 2

	Initials	Date
Prepared By		
Approved By		

WILSON JONES COMPANY   G7514D ColumnWrite ≡

PERSONAL ENERGY AUDIT

MADE IN U.S.A.

DATE	PEOPLE & PROJECTS TO WHOM I GIVE TIME & ENERGY	TOTAL HOURS DONATED	SLEEP & RELAXATION	EATING & FOOD PREPARATION	PERSONAL CARE	INDOOR CLEANING & MAINTENANCE	OUTDOOR GARDENING & MAINT.	
Jan. 1	Talk with Lee	24	8	2	2	1	1	1
2	Wrote in journal	24	9	130	130	1	—	2
3	Did a watercolor	24	8	1	2	3	—	3
4	Visited Lee's Family	24	8	1	1	1	2	4
5	Focused on business	24	830	130	1	30	30	5
6	School, Etc.	24	8	2	2	2	—	6
7	Art project	24	7	1	1	—	—	7
	WEEKLY TOTAL	168	5630	10 —	1030	830	330	8

REVIEW: Are the totals in your Energy Audit what you expected?

SAMPLE

PAGE 1

CLOTHING, SHOES, ETC.	HEALTH CARE	CAR EXPENSES	FUN & GIFTS	LESSONS, BOOKS, ADVANCEMENT	HOUSEHOLD SUPPLIES	OFFICE SUPPLIES	MY NEW CAREER
			5500				
				1015			
—	—	—	5500	1015	—	—	—

choose to provide money for the following goods and services."

SAMPLE

PAGE 2

STUDYING, PRACTICING NEW SKILLS	FUN	TALKING ON THE PHONE	BUSINESS PAPERWORK	PLANNING MY NEW LIFE	ARTISTIC EXPRESSION	MEDITATION	PRIME TIME FOR SIGNIFICANT OTHER PERSON
1	1	35	25	2	2	1	2
2	2	1	2	3	—	—	2
3	1	30	30	1	4	—	—
1	1	30	3	30	—	1	4
—	2	130	6	—	—	30	2
4	1	1	4	—	—	—	1
2	—	2	4	—	6	—	1
13 –	8 –	605	1955	630	12 –	230	11 –

DAILY JOURNAL FOR THE MONTH OF _____
PAGE 3

	Initials	Date
Prepared By		
Approved By		

WILSON JONES COMPANY   G7514D ColumnWrite

RECEIPTS: COLUMNS 2-14

MADE IN U.S.A.

DATE	EXPLANATION OR FROM WHOM INCOME WAS RECEIVED	AMOUNT	SALARY FROM JOB	SIDELINE INCOME	CHILD SUPPORT	GIFTS FROM MOM	TRADE EXCHANGES	
Jan. 1	Overtime Assoc.	100.00	100.00					1
12	Birthday - Mom	25.00				25.00		2
18	refinished furniture	200.00		150.00				3
24	Bday - Uncle Fred	15.00						4
30	My first sale - Sue	15.00						5
31	Overtime Assoc.	100.00	100.00					6
	MONTHLY TOTAL	455.00	200.00	150.00		25.00		7

Review: Do you acknowledge all of the sources you depend upon?

DAILY JOURNAL FOR THE MONTH OF _____
PAGE 4

	Initials	Date
Prepared By		
Approved By		

WILSON JONES COMPANY   G7514D ColumnWrite

PERSONAL ENERGY INCOME

MADE IN U.S.A.

DATE	FROM WHOM OR WHAT ENERGY WAS RECEIVED	TOTAL HOURS RECEIVED	VISITS FROM FRIENDS	EXTRA ATTENTION FROM OTHERS	SPECIAL TIME ALONE	DANCING	LONG HOT BATHS & MASSAGE	
Jan 4	Lee's family	4		2				
7	Art project	6			6			
12	Mom's visit	1						
18	Massage treat	1					1	
24	Uncle Fred	1						
30	Sue	2	2					
31	Needed this!	1					1	
	MONTHLY TOTAL	16	2	2	6	—	2	

Review: Let's hope your perceived income/rewards are greater than this.
The main point is, are you receiving what you want to be receiving from

TAX & OTHER REFUNDS	GARAGE SALES	LOANS	QUICK CASH DEAL	FOOD STAMPS OR GARDEN	GIFTS FROM OTHERS	LOTTERY & OTHER MIRACLES	MY NEW CAREER
	5000						
					1500		
							1500
	5000				1500		1500

SAMPLE
PAGE 4

WATCHING TV	WALKS IN THE PARK	PLAYING WITH CHILDREN	SHOPPING FOR CLOTHES	DOING SPIRITUAL RITUALS	EXERCISING	VISITS FROM RELATIVES	SURPRISES
2							
						1	
						1	
2	—	—	—	—	—	2	—

whom you want to receive it?

121

The worst that could happen is:

The way I might deal with it is:

My security stash must include:

The Grandfathers

Allow the product or service you are providing (or considering providing) to lead you back into history. Research the beginnings of your field. This will not only help you to be an authority, but may prevent you from making the same mistakes others have made in your area. Learn from your grandfathers.

Accomplishment Seventeen - Listen to the Grandfathers

Get acquainted with the past. How has your business been done before? Talk to the elders, read historical accounts, ponder the past.

What was good about it? What was bad? Discover which policies of doing business you want to carry forward.

Even though times have changed, customers still want courteous service and a good value for their money. In Grandfather's day, the local craftsperson or shopkeeper had a reputation to maintain. Neither Grandpa nor the businessperson was planning on leaving town for perhaps the rest of their lives. Today, it is easy to imagine that how you treat a client or customer is not so important because you may never see them again. You or they are likely to be moving on, trying another store, another town, another new possibility. But you want that customer to return, and these days, you may be able to follow them by direct mail no matter where they go. Treat each person as if they were going to live forever in the same town with you.

> *The environmental era calls us back to simpler values. We may use high technology for some of our purposes, but we must make sure this technology is good medicine.*

One of the directions of the 1990's is toward solving environmental problems. Perhaps we would not have so many of these if Grandpa had thought ahead seven generations as our Native American ancestors did. Your business must correct some of Grandfather's oversights. You can help the environment by situating your business where people can reach it on foot, by bicycle or mass transit.

You can create an ambiance around your place of business that makes people feel like stopping by, staying awhile, being nurtured. Plants, benches, sunlight, cozy nooks where people can feel they are making a private decision, and easy access to you, the shopkeeper who has the information they seek, all make your client feel at home. Though each type of business has specialized space requirements, be sure to consider how it would feel to be a stranger entering your domain.

Naturally, you will recycle your waste materials. Conserving resources gives your children's children a chance to inherit the Earth. It has only been in the last generation or two that the adults of industrial society have ended up with little or nothing to pass on to their children. This situation is similar to that of serfs and slaves who worked all their lives with no option of transferring title to land or goods to their children. Technological society has told us to consume based on the assumption that we control all resources, are entitled to use them up, and if we make a mistake, we will invent something better for the future. We can now see the error in this thinking.

As species of plant and animal die out and the medical system fails to foster health in human beings, we must mourn what we have lost. The hopes and promises of the 1950's, the leisure life of tidy families surrounded by labor-saving devices, has come into being for a few at the expense of many. No one then expected homelessness and hunger to be at the top of the list of problems in the 1990's. America had reaped a fertile land, a gift taken from the native Earthkeepers who lived respectfully with nature. The new settlers were hungry for paradise, hardworking, and unfortunately, often shortsighted.

It is natural for a father to want to pass on his wisdom, his profession, his land, and his belongings to his son. It is natural for a mother to want to pass on her wise woman ways, the secrets of her craft, and the riches of her holdings to her daughter. To do so, you must have some. To have some, you must be in business "for yourself" and become debt free. Our foremothers and forefathers had an amazing opportunity: new land, new wealth, new laws on their side giving them rights and power.

But they, as a whole, failed to see themselves in context, failed to think ahead about the effect of their ways upon the future. We can no longer "homestead" by squatting on the acreage of our choice. We cannot freely harvest the wilds. But we can go back to releasing ourselves from financial indebtedness and begin again, this time with greater reverence for nature and nature's people, to work hard in the context of a small round island floating in a great universe.

We can say to ourselves, "I am here now. I have learned from the past." We can make a choice to go in the direction of stability, travelling only the circle of seasons, investing our time and energy into what is before us.

The current technological society is very mobile. It has promoted remortgaging our homes so that we never own them. It has continually promised "greener pastures." It has told us that Grandfather's profession is no longer useful. "You can be whatever you want to be in America," we have been told. "But first," it subtly says, "Spend." Spend for school. Spend for distractions. Spend for the fun of spending. Work harder so that you feel more intensely the need for spending to feel good. Give up your connections to family and childhood friends so that we can sell you a celebrity on TV to replace them. Give up your old hometown for new adventures, none of which are free. Work harder to have more. The carrot is always before your nose.

But what have we given up to get it? Think hard about these things. Think deeply about the quality of life you want to live and what you are willing to give for the rest of your life to live it. Total the balances on your credit cards now. How many years at your present salary will it take you to pay them off? This is how long you have enslaved yourself if you do not make a change right now. Is it worth it? Of all the things you purchased, what will you pass on to your children?

The environmental era calls us back to simpler values. We may use high technology for some of our purposes, but we must make sure this technology is good medicine. Could we invent a computer that lasts a lifetime? Imagine an heirloom car which proudly wears Grandpa's hand-carved hood ornament and Grandma's embroidered seat covers. What if there were fast foods in "Take home and bring back" boxes? How about building materials sized for women's bodies so that any woman could easily build her own house? What if there were a town from which no one moved?

Life could be very different from what it is now. There is plenty of room for innovation and entrepreneuring in our time. I believe that if all of the creative energy of all of the people now working jobs they do not like were liberated, all of the problems of the world could be solved in a year or two. To accomplish this, we must free ourselves to be in business doing what we want the way we want to do it. I assume that is a medicine way because you are a person who cares about the whole world and the fate of the planet.

Reconnect the sacred hoop. Think of past. Think of future. Put yourself in between. You link the two. You are the point of power. You are the only being alive in the position of possible change. You direct which way the world goes by the choices you make today. You are carrying on a heritage. It may not be of your particular family as those bonds have often been severed by modern life. But whatever profession you choose has some history. Whether you link the ancient temple goddesses with the high priestesses of the new age by practicing healing massage or link the ancestral cathedral builders with the architects of dwelling in harmony now, you are the active point.

Put yourself in the context of your profession as it extends through time. Ask yourself, "When I am old, how will I want my work to be remembered?"

Review - Accomplishment Seventeen

Seventeen - Look back to Grandfather's time. What values from the past are needed in the present.
The Grandfathers - What is the heritage left to you? What will you leave your children?
Important Success Tool #17 - A sense of history...knowing his story.

The way I want my work to be remembered is:

I hope to pass on to the next generation, the following:

My Heritage

Family Elders	Profession, lifestyle, skills, or talents:	What they may have to share with me:

The History of Power

There was a time when personal power was measured by how long you survived. Old age depended upon hunting well, gathering and preparing food properly, keeping warm in winter and making no enemies, or at least outsmarting them. As societies became more "civilized" and complex, power became the warrior's domain.

Weapons made him strong. Instead of attuning to the spirit within an animal or plant to summon one's supper, the warrior simply overpowered him. Spirituality moved out of the hands of women who, in many native societies, guided the hunter by her psychic visions and controlled any fighting by making the final decisions about whether a particular battle was worth the losses which would ensue.

Perhaps it was "better" weapons which finally made men feel they no longer needed woman's attunement. There are many theories of how the change came about. Spirituality then moved into the hands of priests who sided with kings who controlled the warriors who used the weapons, and this was how the rule was kept. Now, we have taken the use of force to its extreme where annihilation of all life on Earth including the planet itself is theoretically possible.

As men began to count on dominating by mechanical, industrial, scientific, and technological power, the spiritual life-giving power of woman fell from grace. Their specialty seemed no longer to be needed. It was thought that great inventions would solve all problems and bring about the most wonderful world. Now we know it isn't so.

But it is not so much that the inventions were wrong as that they were created without consulting the female, the positive life-giving force of the universe. The balance was lost as she was deemed no longer useful. Before the time of male dominance, there was an era when life-giving held the highest place. The Goddess was worshiped around the world. The Great Mother lived in peace. Men and women felt the power of her nature to be greater than their own.

Now we have run the course of supposing the inventions of men to be greater than nature. As powerful as human inventions are, I suspect that Mother Earth can still outmaneuver we human beings. Though modern life has done much to foul her atmosphere and body, we are seeing that she stubbornly refuses to give up. A true Medicine Woman, the Earth, living on NO MATTER WHAT.

As we have come to see this, we as women have taken heart. We are not dead yet either. Our power, the power of the feminine nurturing energy, in ourselves and the men who understand us, is on the rise. We feel it in our bones. We feel it in our lives.

Lest we become one-sided here, the power of the male as life-taker, as the one to whom death is not fearsome, must also be restored. Though, in our time, we have seen wanton killing, this is not a recognition of death as a natural transformation. Murder and victimization have nothing to do with ending life respectfully and bringing in new life in thanksgiving.

You are a part of the rebalancing of male and female, in yourself, between men and women, and in society as a whole. You can effect this reestablishment of the sacred attitudes most directly at this point in time by your daily business practices. Through all of the sociopolitical changes since the beginning of time, merchants have been trading, not only goods and services, but points of view, ways of living, and religious attitudes. Merchants in business have wheeled and dealed taking advantage of whatever situation was at hand. So clever, so adept have they become at seizing the moment, that now money is more influential than governments or religious dogma in shaping the world. This is a major shift of power which can easily go unnoticed without a long term historical view.

It was difficult for a woman to be a warrior while she was raising the children and cooking the dinner. It was impossible to rise to the ranks of king and take charge of the kingdom. We all know the problems of getting anywhere in a patriarchal world. But business, which brings us the money system, also brings us the first crack in the structure. Yes, big business has been male-dominated for a long time. But we do not want big business. Sure, some of us do, but not you who are reading this book.

All you need is money. And small business will give you all you want. For our present purposes, money is very important. We can make it subject to our creative, life-giving influence. And we can do it now. The money you earn by your small life-enhancing business venture is the foot-in-the-door of the return of the Goddess. The return of balance to planet Earth. The return of nourishment to women and men and all children to come.

We are not going to go back to the days of living off wild game and berries. That plentiful natural world no longer exists. But we can wield the power of money now to choose by our purchases to support that which brings the world we want. We can choose now by our businesses to create blessings for the planet. As we let our respect for life and love of beauty guide our creations, we can heal and make whole again.

It is time to creatively employ ourselves. It is time to put our real spiritual power, our nourishing, family-making, clan and community forming tendencies to work again in the world. We have been intimidated far too long by the power of dominance, the power of kings, warriors, and priests. Let the men rest. Let them rest in our arms again and in the arms of Great Mother. Let their inventions, and our own, be guided by the life-giving force within.

Affirm: My power is the quality which always and everywhere attracts my good and benefits all life.

Everything you want requires the outpouring of some quality in yourself. To understand this in your own life, complete the following exercise. The thing I want is _____. The quality a person must have if they are to achieve or acquire such a material manifestation is _____. This is the quality you will now develop in yourself to act as a magnet which will draw to you the material manifestation you desire.

Can you initiate the onset of this quality by yourself? If not, what change can you make so that this quality will be activated? Can you maintain this quality by yourself? If not, who can help you? In what circumstances is it appropriate to exhibit this quality? In what circumstances is it inappropriate?

How might this quality change your life for the better? For the worse? What might you lose by acquiring this quality? What might you gain? What prevents you from having this quality now? What does the obstacle look like, feel like, sound like, taste like, smell like? Draw a symbol of the obstacle. What benefits does the obstacle allow you to maintain? How can you replace these benefits in your life?

The quality through which you will transform the obstacle will become your power. Describe this power. How does it feel? What does it sound like? How does it taste and smell? Draw a symbol of the power or find a picture of someone exhibiting this power. What are people like who exhibit this power? List people who will benefit from this new power you develop in yourself.

Once again, look at your resources. What material things do you already have which help you to feel this power or which are reminders of your exhibiting this power in the past? What supports can you supply yourself which will help you maintain this quality? How might you demonstrate this quality in your daily life in a way that others can either see, hear, feel, smell or taste it?

Now that you more thoroughly understand the quality needed to acquire your desired outcome, the thing you want, begin logging your personal acts of power, the expressions of this quality which you decided was needed, on the Power Log chart. Each day, repeat: "I am actualizing the power of _____ in myself." Remember, your creative use of power benefits the world because of the life-affirming choices you make. Each act of your power of _____ brings you closer to your good, the material manifestation of _____ _____ which you believe to be within the realm of benefit to others in the world.

Power Log

Date	Act of Power	Benefit

The Grandmothers

This is the time to be your own grandmother. Mythically speaking, she is the nurturer and caretaker with plenty of time to do just the right thing. She would ask, "How are you feeling?" "Could you use some chicken soup or apple pie?" She worries about your health and makes sure you have the most pleasing medicines for whatever ails you. She does not want you to smoke or drink too much. And your clothes should be clean.

Nothing is too good for her grandchild. Physical, emotional, and spiritual needs are all the same to her. If something troubles you, she is sure that her love mixed with her cooking and a keen eye to your comfort will cure whatever it is.

Her approach is holistic. She knows just when you need a compliment and when to send you home. Now, you are going to look at your life through her eyes.

Accomplishment Eighteen - Care for Yourself

Check your use of substances which alter your state of being: drugs, medicines, alcohol, sex, and spending. Are any of these out of line with the life you want to be living? If so, it is probably because you have lost some of the other comforts Grandmother used to provide. What can you do to get back to that loving touch? Would a weekly massage help? A support group? Think about the pleasure you would prefer to your addiction.

> *Addiction is merely a wrong turn taken by a strong desire for transcendent experience.*

Addiction is merely a wrong turn taken by a strong desire for transcendent experience. Addiction is a narrow road veering off from the path of your creative expression. The more strongly you are addicted, the more likely your creative, spiritual nature could do great things.

Going toward managing your life, taking control of one aspect after another is a liberating experience. Ironically, each act of discipline can bring tremendous feelings of freedom. The change you want to make is merely one of focus. You are substituting new actions for old. It never works to "give up" a pleasure. A healthier or more desirable pleasure must simply be put in place of the old.

If you have been in the habit of handing your power over to a mate or a boss or a substance, that habit can be changed by following the self-empowering exercises in this book. If you are addicted to anything potentially harmful to your self, that addiction can be transferred to an area of creativity where it becomes fuel for

136

developing expertise. Give yourself permission to spend all of the money you now spend on an addictive substance on your creative tools. These might be books, paintbrushes, dancing shoes, rose-covered ledger books, massages, shiny new carpentry tools, or who knows what. Indulge in something which supports your new career.

You are taking charge of your whole life. You are "trading up" in every area of your life. Listen to that Inner Grandmother as she tells you to stand up tall, be proud of yourself. You are beautiful. You are intelligent. You are talented. You can do it. Take whatever steps you must to provide nourishment for your spiritual creative self.

Make a list of any negative addictions you have. Next to each one, write eighteen possible things you would enjoy doing/having instead. Stretch your imagination. Pick the most doable from your list and add them to your mental/emotional/physical diet now. You are going on a diet of holistically nourishing substances. In addition to healthful food, you are now going to allow yourself to take in everything else which nourishes you.

Review - Accomplishment Eighteen

Eighteen - Look at your habits. What would Grandma say?
The Grandmothers - Nourish your wholeness.
Important Success Tool #18 - A diet of holistically nourishing substances.

Nourishments

Present addicting or unsatisfying substance:	Money/time I spend on this false nourishment:	I will exchange for this true nourishment:

Rebirth

If you have carried out your schedule and begun to manage your space, time, and money, a feeling of rebirth will be growing within you. You will sense once again that life is yours. You are a competent, sensitive, balanced person, and you are in business assisting others you enjoy in ways you like and they value.

Accomplishment Nineteen - Feel the Spirit of Rebirth

The medicine wheel of life will continue to turn bringing winter's self-reflection and feeling of aloneness, spring's time of exuberant inspiration, summer's deeply thoughtful planning episodes, and fall's times to just relax and give thanks. Harmonize your energy output with what each season asks of you. Certain times of the year will call you outdoors: the first snow, a day of early blossoms, a summer rain. Be sure to accept nature's invitation to join her in these special events. They are the celebrations she has for you to acknowledge your relationship to her. They are the opportunities for spontaneity in your scheduled life.

> *Harmonize your energy output with what each season asks of you.*

In your business, you may also want to celebrate the seasons. Try to go beyond the usual "end of the season" sale approach. Come up with some fresh ideas. Is there anything you can do to help your customers really enjoy the coming season? What have you ever received from another business which really made you feel as good as new?

Is there any way you can nourish nature while serving your clients? If you continually relate yourself to the planet, you will find ideas planted in your mind that seem to come from her. She is your mother, after all, and her nature is to produce abundance. All you need to do is cooperate. Give your customers the freshness you feel. Make a list of small seasonal pleasures you enjoy. Alongside each, write how you might offer some version of each one to your customers.

Review - Accomplishment Nineteen

Nineteen - List nineteen seasonal treats you might give to your customers.
Rebirth - Feel brand new by letting nature nourish you.
Important Success Tool #19 - Take spontaneous "weather breaks," "whether" or not you are busy, when Nature provides a special event.

Giveaway Pleasures

Seasonal pleasures I enjoy:	I might offer my customers:

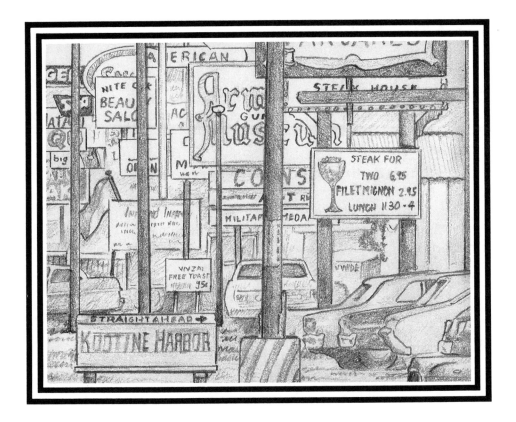

Discernment

Once people notice you are doing things, they will ask you to do more. All sorts of needy folks may knock at your door. If they do not come in person, they will come through the mail. You will want to help. Once you appear successful, every socio-political group will send you a plea. Credit card companies will beg you to apply. Businesses will attempt to lure you with catalogs of diamonds and dreams. Co-workers or supervisors may expect you to do more. Your own desire to progress may push you into accepting more engagements than you have time to fulfill.

New learning opportunities will beckon. A whole new level of trinkets and triumphs will dance before your eyes, seeming to be only a few dollars or hours away. The desire to have them all is strong. These desires are stirred daily by public media. But more is not the equivalent of better.

Accomplishment Twenty - Learn to Discern

Progress is not your most important goal. You want success in your terms, not Madison Avenue's. The only thing you have to do in this life is take care of yourself and relate well to your environment. This is a big enough job under the present circumstances. You may never have been taught the first thing about providing food, clothing, or shelter for yourself at a basic pre-shopping level. You were taught by the culture to consume, and then consume some more. This message is deeper than you think.

The material wealth of the 1950's and 1960's generated a "throw away" philosophy. Our grandparents or great grandparents may have been totally frugal, but we who spent our formative years after World War II in America's burgeoning economy learned to indulge, then toss aside. Over the years, this philosophy has entered into people's relationships with mates, friends, home towns, and the Earth in general.

How often have you heard people say things like, "This town doesn't have anything to offer me anymore." Or, "He just isn't filling my needs any longer." Or, "This degree ought to get me more." The key words, of course, are "get" and "me." The idea of giving your true talents and devoting all of your gifts to any one person, place, or thing is alien to our media-trained minds. But, deep down, we know something is wrong. And now the Earth herself is reminding us. The results of consumerism are coming in. It is not a throw-away world.

The fact that a whole generation or two have lived this way, however, has caused deep psychic hunger. Leaving home, leaving loved ones, leaving one's true self for a so-called better anything produces hunger in the psyche. When the creative aspect of your being is denied, the craving begins. And America offers numerous substances and substitutes for "the real thing."

Your freely flowing alive and creative energy by nature seeks to share in love. Your first task in learning to discern will be to recognize that when this full Self expression is denied, you are programmed to go for a quick fix. Beware of the habit of buying "more, newer, better." It is a dissatisfying substitute for planning an achievable good life for yourself.

When you purchase anything from a home to a new briefcase, ask yourself if you could theoretically be happy with this particular item if you were to have it the rest of your life. Ask just how many and what kind of things do you want to take care of in any one lifetime. Let it sink in that you are the one responsible for maintaining each item. Every thing takes energy as well as gives it, even the most "labor saving" devices.

> *The desire for "things" is a hunger for life.*

All things considered, some purchases will be worth every penny and hour of care. They add beauty, convenience and pleasure to your life. Buy whatever adds the qualities in your life you want strengthened. Steer clear of the instantly consumable binge. You will be stuck with the results of whatever you do and, a relationship, whether it is healthy or unhealthy, is hard to end.

The next time you are about to acquire anything - a new dress, a position on the board of directors, a toaster, a hot fudge sundae, a customer, a product to sell, or a new lover - think beyond, "Can I have this?" to, "Do I want a real relationship with this?" Everything you take on binds you to itself in some way for a long, long time. It captivates your emotional energy. Even when it is gone, you find yourself remembering it, and thereby using your time still involved with it.

Now, let us say you have your own buying habits under control. Your second challenge of learning to discern will come when dealing with other hungry people. These may be the people who really do need a meal and shelter or those who are emotionally starved. Your job is to know what you can give, how often, and to whom. If you reach out too far you can lose your balance. You are striving for a combination of compassion and discernment.

Starving souls are going to come around asking you for what they think will make them feel better. Some of them will truly be hardship cases, victims of discrimination and abuse of all kinds. Your heart will go out to them.

As a sensitive soul, you will want to love and heal them. You will long to fix the problem, to change the world. I wish you could. But you cannot. The world is not fixable by you. If it were, Jesus Christ, Martin Luther King, Gloria Steinem, John Lennon, or any number of worthy people would have fixed it. You were designed to do only a part of the planetary healing that must take place. The part that you can play, and only you can do well, is written upon the sacred scroll inside you. It is your unique mix of talents, abilities, and experiences as you apply them in the business of being yourself.

In business, you can only satisfy the "perceived need" another shares with you. For instance, if a customer wants a new car, you sell her one even if you think she would be better off riding a bicycle. She thinks she needs a car. Your business is providing a good one. If your client wants a new hairdo to make her look beautiful, you do not suggest that she find inner beauty instead. You set her hair because that is where your talent lies and that is the business you are in. There may be ways that you can assist the customer in coming to a new awareness about the need for alternative transportation or finding the Inner Light, but if these are not your business, she will not appreciate the advice.

On the other hand, if you are in a healing profession, a client may come saying, "fix me." You will want to perform the miracle he or she desires. You may even think you know how, because in your mind you can see a perfect reality. But, use restraint. Tell the client exactly what your skills are, the results you have achieved in the past, what they might expect from a treatment, and how he or she might assist the process of becoming well. Once again, do what you can with the talents you have, but do not promise what you cannot do.

There will be times, after working with the customers or clients of your profession, that you will see the larger patterns affecting them all.

146

You will see the influence of a system upon an individual and want to redesign that system. This may be your work. Here again, isolate this one system from the many for the purpose of achieving what only you can do.

To discern is to work within limitations, the limitations of your particular talents and abilities as you extend and develop them. This is plenty of territory. Cover it well and you do your part. Expand into too many areas and you lose your credibility and possibility of success.

You are one cell in the battery of life's energy. But you are not alone. We only "do-it-ourselves" with a lot of help from others. You need your clients. They need you. You run your business successfully to the extent that other businesses you depend upon are run successfully. We are interdependent. As we do well what we love to do and share generously within the limitations of our means, everyone is strengthened.

Take on the challenges you must in order to excel, but realize that every new person, place, or thing is a relationship which will pull your heartstrings. How many good-byes do you want to have to say? And how many hellos that signify starting over? Become aware of this hunger chain in yourself and in the people you serve. Break it by discernment.

You bond, to some extent, with everyone and everything you touch. This bond becomes a bind when you touch too many too much. With over accumulation of "stuff" and "things to do" your equilibrium is thrown off. But when you choose your involvements carefully, the bonds you make are positive and wholesome, such as the bond of person to family, person to place, and person to her creative tools and their outcome. If you realize ahead of time that everything you touch, in a sense, sticks to you, you will become careful - discriminating - in your involvements. This may be the hardest lesson to learn if you have been born in America.

Discernment is the quality of knowing how much to take on, who you are capable of dealing with, and whether your skills are useful in a particular situation. If your judgement was discerning, you will acquire only those relationships to people or things of which you can be a proper caretaker. If you simply acquire things to "have" them, you will soon want to throw them away. They will eventually feel like clutter in your life. If what you have is human, she or he will object to being "had" or "owned" or "treated like a piece of property." If you "have" customers, pretty soon they will go where someone "relates" to them instead.

As you develop discernment, you will feel less "used" yourself. The people to whom you do relate will feel alive and rich in the relationship because you consciously chose them and have the ability to work with them. The material things to which you relate will take on the patina of your loving care.

Whenever you are asked to come into relationship with another person or thing, look at your calendar. Do you have time for the actual process for which you are contracting? What can you offer? What are the limits of your time and energy?

Once you are clear with yourself about this, you will be clear with others. You are taking command of your life now; things you enjoy are scheduled in. There is only so much room for more. When the calendar is full, you are full. Opening new times and spaces requires closing out old activities, bringing client relationships to firm completion, and ending unsatisfactory commitments.

Discernment is a very refined quality. It is taking your art to its highest form. The benefits of acquiring discernment are long-term, fulfilling relationships between you and everyone you know and daily enjoyment of all the things of which you have decided to become steward. It may also mean that you find yourself staying in one place, passing up "the chance" to move even for more money. It may mean you get to enjoy a twenty year garden or walk down the street and have everyone know your name. You may gain a solid reputation for whatever you do in your local area. It might mean you stay with one mate or end up with a vintage car and a house on the historical register.

You may not feel like spending a lot of money. Who knows, you might find no need for TV. Your bicycle may be all the transportation you need. The place where your kids play might be the same place you played as a child. Life could be very different. Even while we send communications around the world, we must realize that the need to actually touch - in the flesh touch - our friends and our past is real. We <u>can</u> break the chain of want/get/have that leads to emotional starvation.

The desire for "things" is a hunger for life. Fewer products may be sold if we partake of life fully; and, therefore, your business may not earn you a fortune, but you are prepared. Your basic security stash is ready. The Seed Vision inspires a plan that gives you one direction to go. As soon as you manifest any part of this plan, you have "arrived." The life "out there somewhere" begins to be here, now.

Meanwhile, the other hungry people still call out for help. If you give to them from the well of talent inside you and touch them with your thoughtful concern, they will begin to be healed. They will feel your warmth and come back again and again until they, too, have been empowered to form relationship. Your life becomes an example of living nourishment. In business for yourself, you form the core of a new world that will take shape around you. Meet your real need. Stop the hunger. These are the results of discernment.

Review - Accomplishment Twenty

Twenty - Look at each thing you have; describe your relationship to it.
Discernment - Know when to say "no."
Important Success Tool #20 - The power to hold still.

A recent situation where I could have used discernment is:

What I might have done differently is:

Learning to Discern

Kinds of people/things I want to be in relation to:	Kinds of people/things I want to avoid:

Dancer

As the days go by, you are meeting the appointments you have made on your calendar. Your home and work space should be taking shape. You are creating rituals for releasing frustrations as well as actually getting rid of useless things which take up your time and energy. You continue to observe yourself, your desire to achieve your Seed Vision, and you make any slight adjustments until the Vision is totally compelling. This gives you enthusiasm that takes you through your daily tasks. You are giving yourself treats and taking time to relax. No matter what job you are currently working, life ought to be feeling a lot better.

If by now you know this job is the right job for you, skip ahead to

Accomplishment Twenty-One. If you are still trying to create a job based on your true talents, read on. The job you create, either as self-employment or employment for Self, can be looked at as a dance. You are the choreographer. You have a feel for the general flow, can imagine a couple of spectacular movements, perhaps, but now it is time to take it step by step.

If you do not already have a particular business in mind, I suggest you read <u>What Color is Your Parachute?</u> by Richard Nelson Bolles. This is the best text I have ever seen for helping you to figure out how your talents and tendencies fit into the current job market. Do all of the exercises in the book. They help you to redescribe yourself and open your mind to positions you may never before have considered.

To help you find your true work, make several 3" x 5" cards which ask the question: "How might I support myself while doing what I love?" Hide these cards in places where you least expect them, such as, in a book you will be reading, on your closet door, taped to the back of your cereal box, in the cookie jar, etc. Whenever you come across a card, spontaneously answer the question. Your subconscious will be informing you of what you really want to be doing.

You can also make a Life Purpose card and attach it to your Seed Vision where you can see it often. To do this, list three of your outstanding skills, talents or character traits. List two or three ways you enjoy sharing these qualities. Describe your highest hopes for others in the world. Combine these into one statement. An example might be: "My purpose is to use my dedication, artistic ability and calmness through my writing and ritual events to liberate creativity in others so that together we might heal the world." Or, you might say, "I love building houses which give beauty to the world and I have the strength and design skill to do it."

Read the Life Purpose card every day. It not only keeps you on track but gives you just the right thing to say when others ask, "What do you do?" It is the best kind of self-promotion.

If you already know yourself and are crafting away at your chosen career but want to focus more intently on achieving your Seed Vision goals, keep up the exercises in this book. Pay particular attention to your market, the people you have chosen to serve. What do they think they want? What are they ready for? Is there a way to revamp your product or service to more clearly fill the bill? Continue to fine tune yourself to your people. Ask them questions. Give them little extras if they choose you over a competitor. Your dance has to look a little more fun.

Keep close track of your income and outgo. Yes, every day, and every day and every day. Slice off unnecessary time and energy expenses. Be ruthless. And add on pieces of your Seed Vision as simply and as quickly as you can. Think about the great dancers you have seen. One thing they all have in common is that their act is crisp and clean, no sloppy movements, no wasted motion. Tuck it in! Practice! Perfect that which you are putting out. When you are doing your job, do it well. Be demanding of yourself. When work is over, enjoy and rest.

> *Your way of earning a living must be a living. It must be alive with all of your spirit invested in every detail.*

Remember the balance. A dance is all about balance. Your music, the inner song which moves your life, will be different than everyone else's, but it will contain the elements of harmony. This life is your work of art and you must treat it as such.

Think of the intricate beadwork, weaving, or painted pottery of tribal people. Every practical item was a work of art. Look at the still standing cathedrals, centuries old structures, and know that the builders thought of their work as much more than a job. Your way of earning a living must be a living. It must be alive with all of your spirit invested in every detail.

Moreover, think of your work as a Life Work, not a week's work, not two year's work, but a LIFE'S WORK. Take the time to do it right. It will never be done until your life is done. It is your major act of power in this lifetime. It is your life dance. Make it sweet. Make it sensual. Make it exciting. Meet the people you most want to meet with it. Entertain your family with it. Heal the world with it. Make it worth your while to do it as long as you live. This is how important it is.

Then, you will feel like dancing!

Accomplishment Twenty-One - Be a Dancer

Now, congratulate yourself. You have made significant inner changes. Perhaps huge outer changes. So, take a shower. Use your favorite soap. Dress up in your best. Invite a fun companion and go dancing. Or do whatever, in your opinion, symbolizes success, whatever makes you feel on top of the world. You have it all and you are giving your all, living every moment.

You are looking outside yourself to notice and respond to the needs of others and your planet. You are rich with awareness. You are moved by your own passions. You are affected by life. You are fired up and ready for anything. You know what you can give and have acquired the skills to get it from inside idea to outer manifestation. You are a doer. Whether that doing is as a keeper or a changer, you have the power to accomplish your goals.

And you know when to quit, when to end, to let go, to lighten up, relax, release. You are able to receive, take in, allow, enjoy. You are secure. Your basic needs are met. You have money in the bank. You know where you are going. You are on your way.

Neither God nor nature is forgotten in your plan. You know what you love and what nourishes love. You feel love's Source. You have demonstrated the power to gather love to yourself by gathering the things you love and taking loving care of them. You have learned also to let go in a ritual of loving completion. You have experienced the exquisite emptiness of holding on to nothing unloved. You know the fullness of that state of being.

Your carefully following the prompting of this book and the longings of your soul have brought you here. I have done my part as fully as I could, and you have done yours. It has been a good relationship. Unless, for your own sense of completion, you want to drop me a note on how far you have come, we are ended now.

Though much is to come.

Be blessed on your journey. Use your tools. Follow the Medicine Wheel of Life. Aho!

Review - Accomplishment Twenty-One

Twenty-One - Two and One make twenty-one. Two is for the relationship you have formed to each other being and thing. One is the Real You, the One inside that has found a way out.

Dancer - Your work is the dance of your life. Make it great.

Important Success Tool #21 - The ability to continue, no matter what.

I can make my work

sweeter by

more sensual by

more exciting by

more fulfilling by

more peaceful by

more relaxing by

more enjoyable by

more spiritual by

more ecological by

more fun by

more inspiring by

special by

more lucrative by

more precise by

more desirable by

My work is never done, and I would not have it any other way.

About the Author, Carol Bridges

Born into the post World War II American Dream, I lived an increasingly prosperous childhood while my father went from gas station attendant to corporate president. All of my elder male relatives were small-time entrepreneurs.

My own first jobs were secretarial, although my talent was in the artistic realm. My interests expanded into sociological and psychological fields as I became aware of America's shortcomings. While raising three children, I went to college.

I worked in a crisis intervention center, led personal growth groups and lived communally. Becoming disappointed in the mental health field, I chose to get as far outside society as I could. As a spiritual step, I entered voluntary poverty, giving up a six bedroom home with all the furnishings and choosing to live on the road in a Volkswagen van while I searched for utopia.

I supported myself as an artist until an accident facilitated my interest in healing. My next entrepreneuring venture was starting a school of the healing arts.

In eight years I acquired two homes, a cook, a cleaning woman, and six employees. Then, I lost everything by trying "prosperity consciousness," the think yourself rich philosophy of the new age.

On the way to bankruptcy, I met a man who owned over 100 businesses, a multimillionaire entrepreneur named Ed. Ed had done with money what I had hoped to do with love. He had formed successful work communities of helpful people under the guise of business. I had tried all my life to create community, and it had always suffered from lack of funds. I decided to use business as a healing tool.

Now, I assist heart-centered people in passing through transitions positively, helping them reclaim their full power creatively, spiritually, and in business. In my work to accomplish this, I use all of my talents as artist, dancer, and spiritual guide, as well as every bit of business experience I have accumulated.

I operate a publishing and mail order business and have authored several books including **The Medicine Woman Inner Guidebook, The Medicine Woman Tarot**, and **Secrets Stored In Ecstasy**. My books are distributed internationally and I do workshops across the country.

My nineteen years of private practice holistic counseling and study with native teachers combines with all of my life experience to give me a strong sense of your needs as compassionate human beings struggling to make a good world against all odds. I have been deeply moved by the courage you have shown throughout the intense challenges modern life can bring.

It is my dream to facilitate a healthy community of people whose creativity has been liberated and which is directed toward lifting the burdens of the world. I believe we can restore the planet if we act upon our sense of beauty and wonder again. To this end, I am dedicated.

Business and money will not last forever; we must always be aware of that which is eternal. But, we can use the monetary system as a servant to that which we know to be true and everlasting, the God within all life.

About the Illustrator, Dwight Sands

When I met Carol in 1984, I had a minimum wage job sanding in a furniture maker's shop. Probably because she fell in love with me, she could see I had many talents I was not using then.

I, too, had become disenchanted with the status quo. I was living very simply in a run-down little house on communal land. My goal was to move into an earth lodge I was building - something like a Native American hogan - grow some food and offer my life as a gesture to the Great Mother in a world I thought was beyond help.

Though our love story - Carol's, the Spirit's, and mine - is very beautiful, that is not what I want to share with you now. Let me just say, in the course of our deepening involvement, I was able to observe the ways of being she practiced every day. Whether she was on the verge of losing her home or riding a wave of success, she was always in there learning, reading everything she could about whatever she was focused on, trying out creative ideas, bringing every fantasy as far as she could into material form. And then starting on the next thing!

I saw, over time, that whatever product or service she came up with, even if it sat around for years, would eventually sell. But she did not sit around waiting to see. She would go straight ahead toward her dreams. All the while, she encouraged me to fully utilize my own talents.

I took the plunge into entrepreneuring one day by going to a local toy shop and telling the owner that I could produce a better catalog than the one he was currently using. He liked my sample drawings and was willing to give me a try. We have been working successfully together now for three years.

Freelancing has given me the time to pursue my love of sculpting. I hand carve stone ceremonial pipes and continue exploring art, photography, music, and sculpture. I still live simply. But now my business allows my art and spirit to be offered to others far more expansively than it ever could have been before.

I still garden and love the woods. But I feel what I call "merchant energy" was a part of myself that I tried to avoid. Once I decided it was one of life's powers, I could bring it into balance in myself. I recognize it as the power to make clear contracts, agreements which benefit me and my human brothers and sisters.

I do not plan to ever become "big business" with a lot of employees and paperwork. I plan only to keep doing what I love to do and letting some of my talents express in a commercially acceptable form so that many people can be inspired by the images which flow through me and so that I have the necessary support to build the life which nourishes me and others of this planet.

I grew up on a Navajo reservation and spent several years living in Los Angeles, California. I know the extremes of poverty and wealth, of wild natural space and crowded civilization. I knew somewhere there had to be a balance. Now, I have found it.

Additional Resources

Business Mastery, A Business Planning Guide For Creating a Fulfilling, Thriving Business and Keeping It Successful, Cherie Sohnen-Moe, Sohnen-Moe Associates.
Designed for healing arts professionals, but suitable for any small business.

College Degrees By Mail, John Bear, Ph.D., Ten Speed Press.
100 of the best schools offering degrees entirely through home study. Includes Bachelor's, Master's, Doctorates, and Law degrees. Also lists diploma mills to avoid.

The Designer's Commonsense Business Book, Barbara Ganim, North Light Books.
The most helpful resource for anyone in the graphic arts field. Covers marketing, taxes, forms, and all of the author's hard-won knowledge.

How to Make and Sell Your Own Record, Diane Sward Rapaport, available through Ladyslipper Music Distributers.
The bible for the beginning recording artist. Covers recording, manufacturing, promotion, distribution, and more. If music is your art, you must read this book.

In the Absence of the Sacred, the Failure of Technology and the Survival of the Indian Nations, Jerry Mander, Sierra Club Books.
Read this before you make your next decision involving technology.

Small Time Operator, How to Start Your Own Small Business, Keep Your Books, Pay Your Taxes, and Stay Out of Trouble, Bernard Kamoroff, CPA, Bell Springs Publishing Company.
Very clear directions on business basics.

What Color Is Your Parachute? A Practical Manual for Job-Hunters & Career Changers, Richard Nelson Bolles, Ten Speed Press.
Discovering your skills, where to use them, and how to find the person who will hire you. This is an annual; get the current year's edition.

Index